VIENNA UP CLOSE

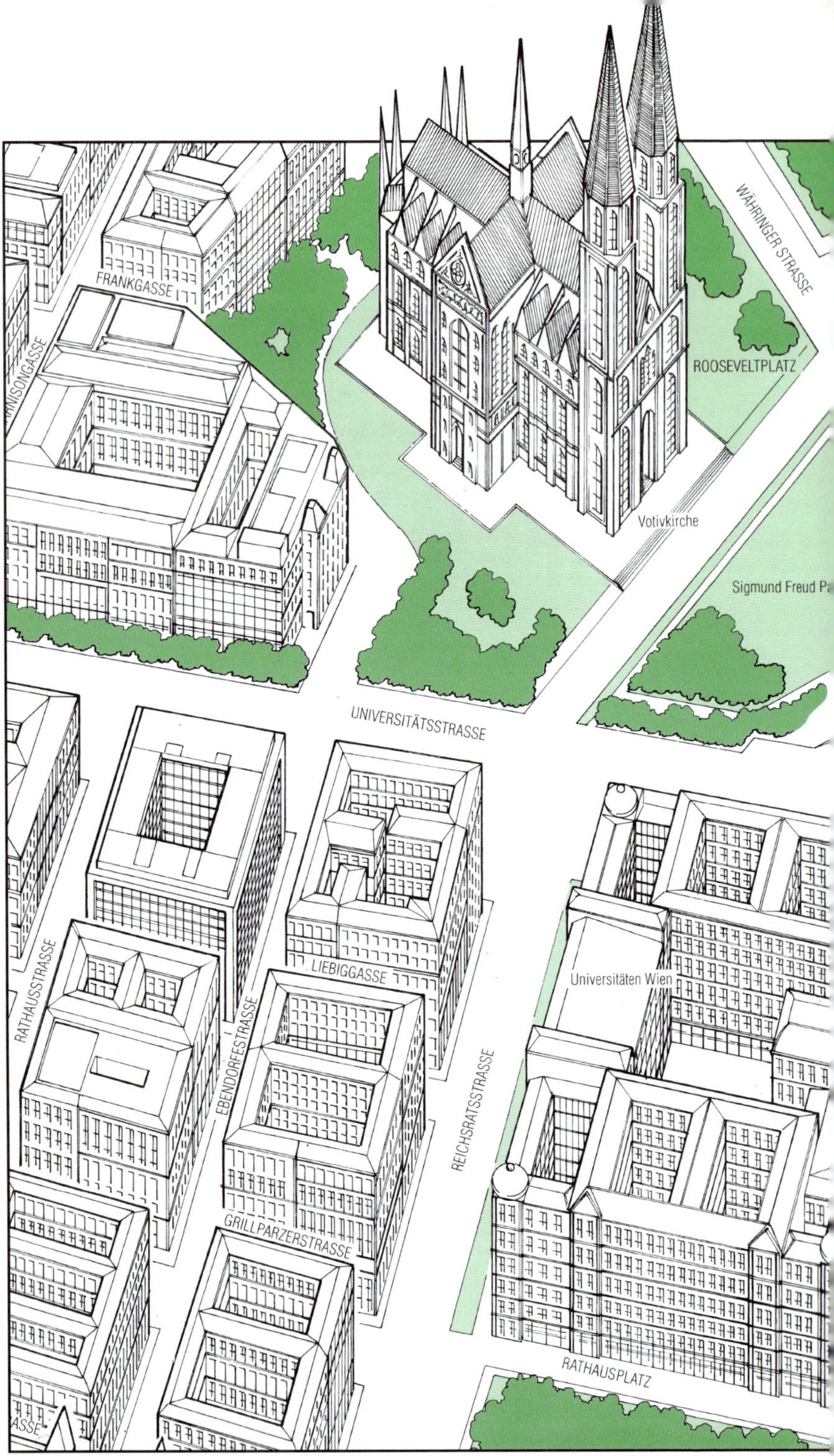
FRANKGASSE
WÄHRINGER STRASSE
ROOSEVELTPLATZ
Votivkirche
UNIVERSITÄTSSTRASSE
RATHAUSSTRASSE
LIEBIGGASSE
EBENDORFERSTRASSE
REICHSRATSSTRASSE
Universitäten Wien
GRILLPARZERSTRASSE
RATHAUSPLATZ

VIENNA UP CLOSE

DISTRICT BY DISTRICT, STREET BY STREET

Written by Louis James
Maps created by John Richards

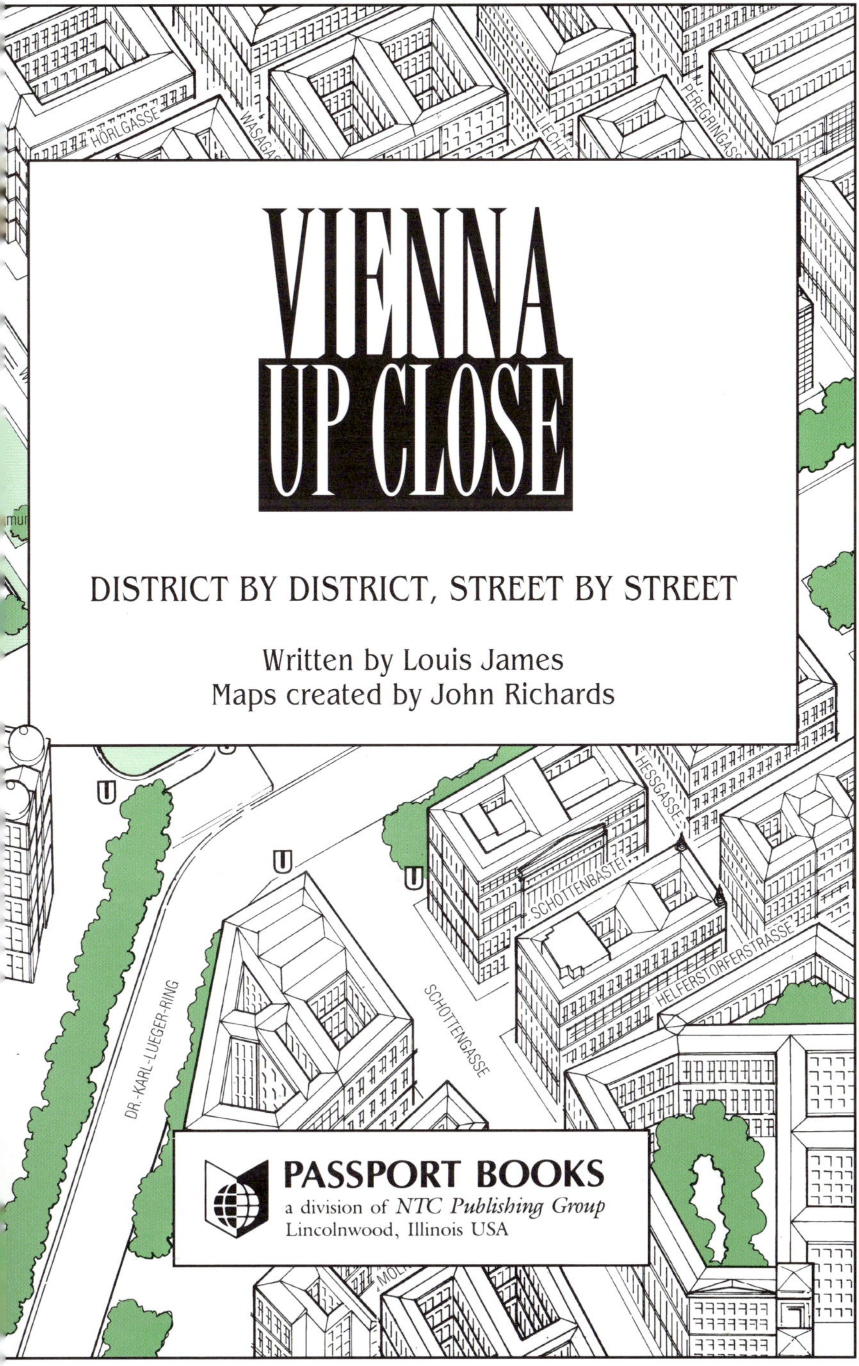

PASSPORT BOOKS
a division of *NTC Publishing Group*
Lincolnwood, Illinois USA

This edition published 1996 by Passport Books,
Trade Imprint of NTC Publishing Group, 4255 West Touhy Avenue,
Lincolnwood (Chicago), Illinois 60646-1975 U.S.A.

Conceived, edited and designed by
Duncan Petersen Publishing Ltd,
31, Ceylon Road,
London W14 OYP

Originated by Reprocolor International, Milan, Italy
Printed by GraphyCems, Navarra, Spain
Cover photo: Austrian National Tourist Office

Library of Congress Catalog Card Number 96-68771

ACKNOWLEDGEMENTS

Editorial

Editorial director	Andrew Duncan
Assistant editor	Nicola Davies
Design	
Art director	Mel Petersen
Designers	Chris Foley and Beverley Stewart
Aerial survey by	Luftreportagen, Vienna
Maps created by	John Richards

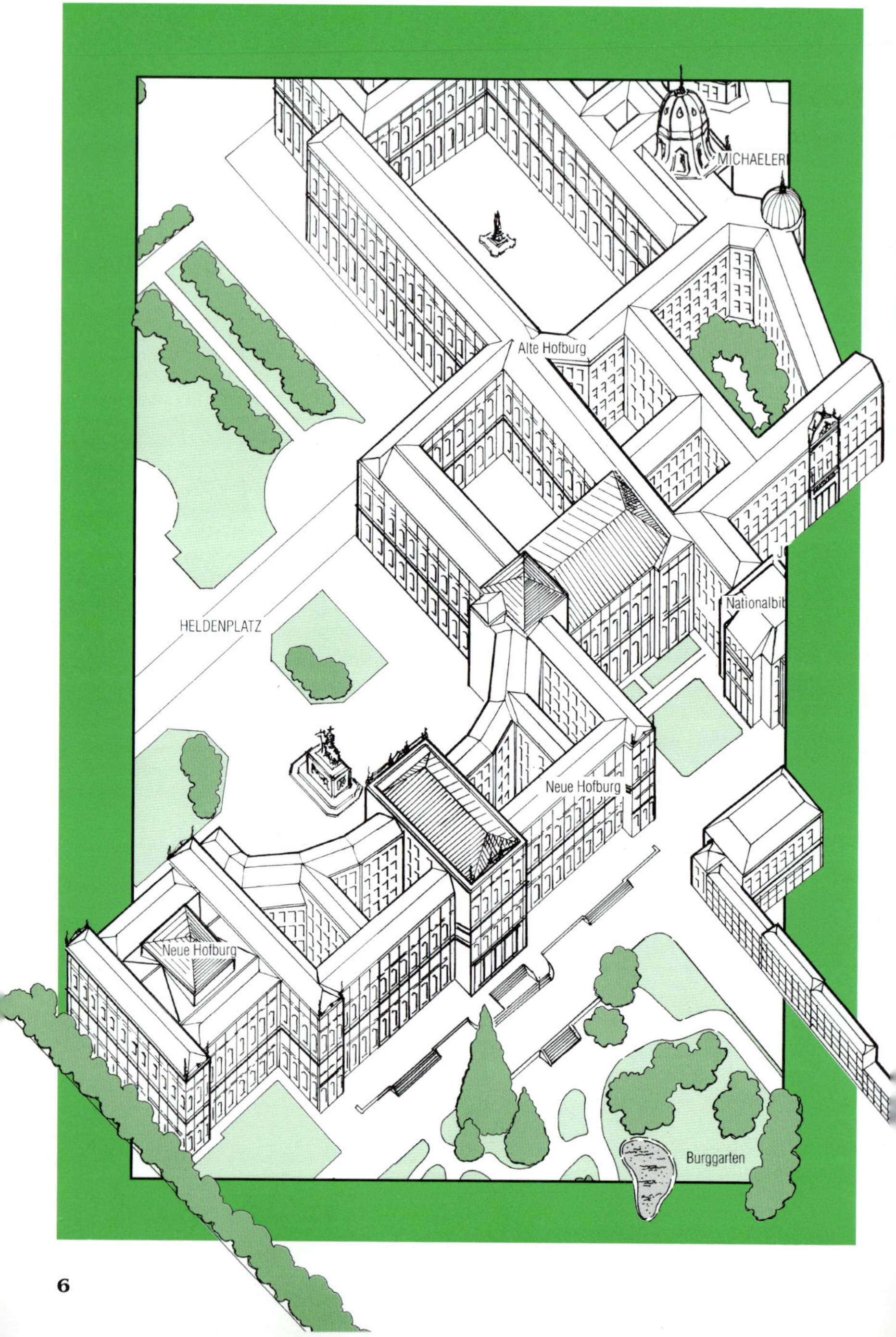
MICHAELER
Alte Hofburg
HELDENPLATZ
Nationalbib
Neue Hofburg
Neue Hofburg
Burggarten

Contents

The indexes are essential features of these guides. In particular, **the index of points of interest** provides, under convenient and obvious headings such as shops, museums, cafés, bars and restaurants, a quick-reference listing of essential practical and sightseeing information: instant access to the guide and to the city.

About this book

How the mapping was made

Isometric mapping is produced from aerial photographic surveys. For this book, aerial photography was provided by Luftreportagen Florian Hausman.

Scores of enlargements were made from the negatives, which John Richards then used to complete the task.

Isometric projection means that verticals are the same height, whether in the foreground or in the background – at the 'front' (bottom) of the page or at the 'back' (top). Thus the diminishing effect of perspective is avoided and all the buildings, whether near or distant, are shown in similar detail and appear at an appropriate height.

The order of the maps

The map squares are arranged in sequence, running from north to south and from west to east. For further details, see the master location map on page 28.

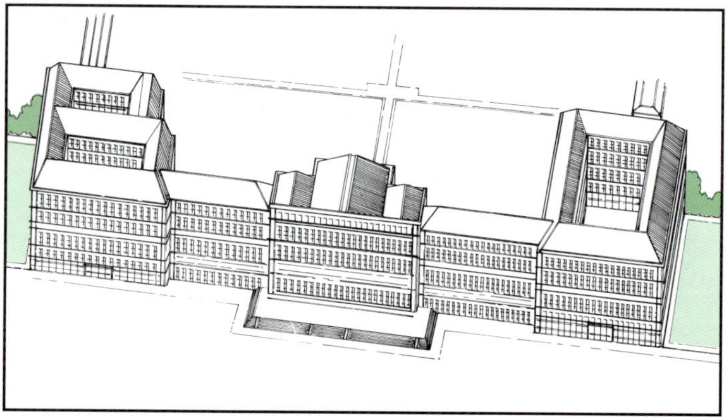

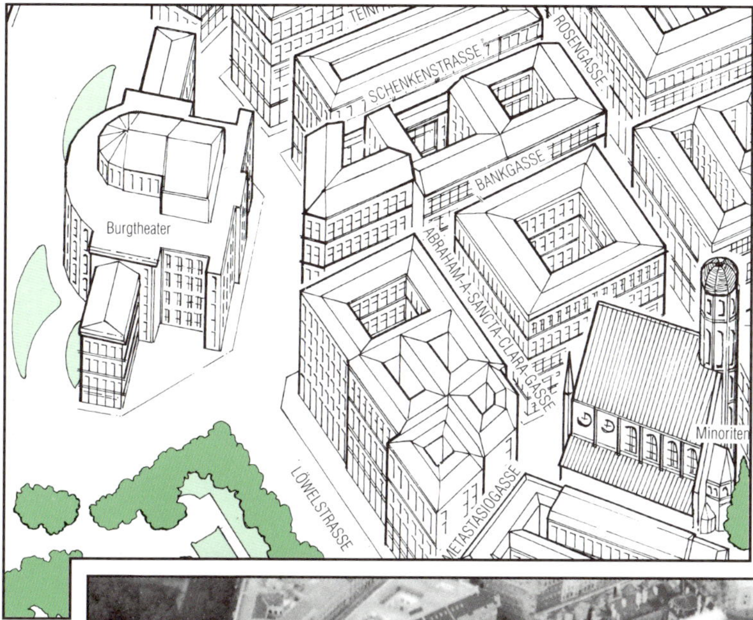
SCHENKENSTRASSE
ROSENGASSE
BANKGASSE
Burgtheater
ABRAHAM-A-SANCTA-CLARA-GASSE
LÖWELSTRASSE
METASTASIOGASSE
Minoriten

Numerals on maps
Each numeral on a map cross-refers to the text printed on the facing page. Generally, features of interest are grouped together, and follow the line of a walk across the map square linking the points of interest. You can visit the highlights of each square in this way, or randomly.

Opening and closing times Unless indicated otherwise in the text, opening times generally follow these rules: Shops open between 8 am and 6 pm (until noon or 1 pm on Saturdays, except for the first Saturday in the month, when (most of them) stay open to 5 or 6 pm). Banks are open 8 am to 12.30 pm and 1.30 pm to 3 pm, late opening Thursday to 5.30 pm. Banks in the city centre might not close for lunch. Museums vary, but most are open 9 am to 5 pm, closing one day in the week, usually Monday.

Prices Restaurants

S	means one person can eat for up to 200 Austrian shillings
SS	means one person can eat for 200-350 Austrian shillings
SSS	means one person generally pays more than 350 Austrian shillings

These prices are for a meal without wine.

Top restaurants such as the Korso offer
menus of AS790 to 900 so the SSS category is wide.

Hotels

S means one person pays 750 to 1,500 Austrian shillings per night

SS means one person pays 1,500 to 2,500 Austrian shillings per night.

SSS means one person pays more than 2,500 Austrian shillings per night.

These prices are for a double room, usually with shower and breakfast-inclusive.

Hotels in Vienna generally have a wide range of room prices and charge a supplement of 25 per cent or more in the summer season and over Christmas and New Year.

Coverage No guidebook can cover everything of interest in Vienna. This one contains a particularly wide range of information, and the writer has concentrated on aspects of the city brought out by the special nature of the mapping, with emphasis on architecture, and on historical and general information that helps to explain the fabric, evolution and working of the city. He has also tended to draw attention to the unusual, even the peculiar, as well as the obvious and well established, in the belief that this best reveals the essential character of a city.

Vienna is unusual among cities in having an exceptional number of major sights concentrated in the ancient core of the city. For this reason, several map squares are featured twice, with different points of interest marked on each.

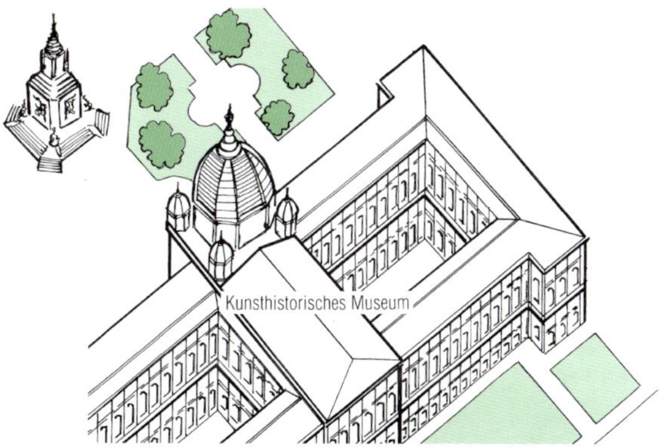

Vienna in a nutshell: the sights you should not miss

These two pages give you instant access to the city. Listed are the 'musts' for every visitor to Vienna, plus the map pages where you'll find the sights marked, together with descriptions linked to the maps by numerals in circles. No such list can pretend to be complete, or to give a fair picture of a city, but if you have limited time, it will help you get the best from Vienna.

This book can, however, give you something more than easy access to the major attractions. The way to get to know a city is, of course, to wander the streets, with no great purpose except to enjoy what comes up. This guide is ideal for that, for highlighted on the maps are all the features, well-known and little-known, that make Vienna special.

Even if you don't feel like walking, just make your way to one of the map squares, find somewhere to sit, and read the maps, with their accompanying text. This is as near as you can get to drifting over the city in a balloon, with your own private guide to describe the points of interest.

Don't miss:

The **Ankeruhr** on the Hohen Markt, ⑥ **pages 55**, is an ingenious historical clock. Be there at noon to see figures from the Viennese past parade across the clockface.

The **Augustinerkirche,** ③ **page 63** , is notable for containing the hearts of the Habsburg rulers, kept in silver urns; also for a magnificent tomb of Maria Theresa's daughter by Antonio Canova.

The **Belvedere,** ① **pages 119–121,** is the finest Baroque palace in Vienna and also contains the Austrian Gallery's paintings by such renowned artists as Gustav Klimt and Egon Schiele.

Figlmüller, ⑤ **page 57**, is the most famous eaterie for Wiener Schnitzel; the biggest versions they serve are claimed to be the size of a lavatory seat.

Graben, ③ **page 53**, once the protective ditch of the Roman camp of Vindobona, is now the most fashionable street in town. Just off it is Hildebrandt's architectural masterpiece, the **Peterskirche, 21**.

The **Hofburg,** ② **page 61**, was the Habsburg centre of power for more than six centuries, in the course of which it was continually enlarged. In the **Winterreitschule** the Lipizzaners give their unique shows and in the **Burgkapelle** the Vienna Boys' Choir performs sung masses on Sundays.

The **Kapuzinergruft,** ② **page 67**, is the imperial vault and has magnificent Baroque tombs.

Karlskirche, ③ **page 115**, is the loveliest Baroque church in Central Europe and the greatest work undertaken by the Fischer von Erlach, father and son.

The riches of the **Kunsthistorischen Museum,** ① **page 59**, would take days to explore: pick your favourite artists from among the greatest of Europe and spend a few peaceful hours there.

Find time to visit the **medieval and Baroque wine cellars**. It was once said that as much of Vienna was below ground as above it: ④ **page 57**, and others – look for the word *Keller*.

One of the most interesting (and pioneering) buildings by the *Secession's* leading architect, Otto Wagner, is his functional **Postsparkassenamt,** ⑤ **page 89**.

Schloss Schönbrunn, ① **pages 124–125**, was Maria Theresa's beloved family home, and its park is equally beloved by the Viennese.

The great Viennese art rebellion of the 1890s began before the **Secession,** ③ **page 103**, was built, but it was here that the rebels subsequently held a series of epoch-making exhibitions that revolutionised the art scene in Austria.

Stephansdom, ⑤ **page 53**, is still for many Viennese the focus of their affections and the symbol of their history. The cathedral is a marvel of Gothic grace that manages also to retain an element of parish-church homeliness.

Getting away from it all

The Viennese have two cherished forms of escapism – walking in the **Wienerwald** and sitting (sometimes singing) in the *Heurigen* (taverns) of the wine-villages on the periphery of the city. Both the woods and the villages are relatively easy to reach from the city centre by tram or by bus. It is certainly worth spending an afternoon or evening in the picturesque villages of **Neustift am Walde, Grinzing** or **Heiligenstadt**, sampling the young wine and enjoying a simple meal of cold meat and cheese. If you are travelling with **children** there is another alternative: the famous **Prater** with its fun-fair. The ride on the big wheel (where Harry Lime contemplated throwing his friend to his death) provides unforgettable views of Vienna. There is a direct metro connection (U1), and these outlying areas are covered by Vienna street maps such as *Falk*.

By tram around the Ringstrasse

One way to get an introduction to Vienna is to travel the circular Ringstrasse by tram. The sights to look out for, clockwise from Schwedenplatz, are:

Radetzky Monument (see a street map such as *Falk*), Österreichisches Museum für Angewandte Kunst – ⑦ on page 97, Stadtpark, ① on page 94, Hotel Imperial, ⑦ on page 105, Staatsoper, ① on page102, Kunsthistorisches Museum, ① on pages 59, Naturhistorisches Musem, ④ on page 93, Parlament, ③ on page 43, Rathaus, ① on page 43, Burgtheater, ① on page 45, Universität, ④ on page 87, Votivkirche, ① on page 33, Börse, ① on page 37.

TRANSPORT

From airport to city

You can travel the 17 km into the city from Vienna International Airport at Schwechat by shuttle bus, direct rail link or taxi.

One shuttle bus runs between the City Air Terminal (beside the Hilton Hotel) and the airport from 6 am to 9 pm, leaving at intervals of between 20 and 30 minutes. The journey usually takes 20-25 minutes.

A second shuttle service runs between the Westbahnhof (West Railway Station) and the airport, stopping at the Südbahnhof (South Railway Station) on the way. It operates between 6 am and 9.15 or 9.30 pm, generally at hourly intervals, and takes about 20 or 30 minutes, depending on where you board. The fare for both buses is AS70 (1995).

A few of the large hotels have their own pick-up service – ask your travel agent if you can take advantage of this.

The rail connection (Schnellbahn) to the airport is from Wien Nord (via Wien Mitte) and Wien Mitte (Landstrasse), running between 5.09 am and 9.45 pm, generally at hourly intervals. (The Landstrasse terminus is close to the city centre and the Hilton.) The last train from the airport leaves at 9.30 pm. It takes 30 to 40 minutes.

Taxis cost a minimum of AS350 to destinations in the city centre, but your fare could be considerably greater if you are going to a western suburb.

It is prudent to allow extra time in the morning, or evening rush

TERMS USED IN THIS GUIDE

A number of architectural terms are used repeatedly; some have a special meaning in the context of Vienna.

Romanesque The earliest form of church architecture, flourishing from the 11thC to the beginning of Gothic.

Gothic Pointed arches and ribbed vaults, mainly of churches: in Vienna, from the 13thC to the mid 16thC.

Renaissance The comparatively short period from the middle of the 16thC to the end. The Stallburg wing of the Hofburg is a mainstream example. Renaissance buildings often had fine courtyards and loggias.

Baroque Palaces and churches, all sweeping vistas, elegant domes and sumptuously theatrical ornamentation; early 17thC to late 18thC.

Neo-Classicism Embodying classical forms such as columns and pediments, the favoured style between the late 18thC and 1840.

Historicism Revamping and reproducing the great styles of the past to produce Neo-Renaissance, Neo-Gothic and Neo-Baroque buildings. Lasted from the mid 19thC to the end of that century.

Jugendstil An exotic, flowing and sensual architectural style, beginning in Vienna in 1897 amd lasting until around 1910. The local version of Art Nouveau.

Post-modern Contemporary architecture. Usually characterized by extensive use of colour and 'quotations' from earlier styles. In Vienna, mainly used for hotels.

hours if you are travelling by bus or taxi.
For airport information, tel. 711 10 22 31.

Independent travel to Vienna

By rail Vienna is about 22 hours by rail from London and 11 hours from Cologne. The three international railway stations have information and accommodation bureaux, exchange counters which are not limited to banking hours (but are not 24-hour), and a choice of taxi, tram and U-Bahn connections to destinations within the city.

By car Tourist information is available as you approach Vienna on the Westautobahn (A1) at the Wien-Auhof exit, open from 8 am to 10 pm in summer and from 9 or 10 am to 6 or 7 pm in the winter. At the Südautobahn (A2) exit there is also an information bureau: you will find it at Autobahnabfahrt Zentrum, Triester Strasse 149, open in summer between 8 or 9 am and 7 or 10 pm, closed between November and March.

Geography

Vienna has 23 districts/(*Bezirke*) arranged (roughly) in two concentric circles fanning out from the centre. The Innere Stadt ('inner city') is the oldest part and constitutes the first district. The Innere Stadt is enclosed by the Ringstrasse, built in the 19thC as a showcase of Historicist architecture, epitomizing the wealth and self-confidence of capitalism and the new rich. District 2, Leopoldstadt, is across the Danube Canal from the Innere Stadt and was the Jewish quarter until the Nazi deportations. Districts 3 to 9 lie between the Ringstrasse and Vienna's outer ring road, the Gürtel, while numbers 10-23 lie beyond the Gürtel, stretching out gradually to the wine villages and the Wienerwald (Vienna Woods) in the south, west and north-west, or lying beyond the Danube to the north (numbers 21 and 22). (Postal codes have four figures, all starting with 1; the middle two figures indicate the district. Thus the first district is 1010, the tenth is 1100, and the nineteenth 1190.)

The first-time visitor to Vienna will perhaps be disappointed to discover that the northern perimeter of the Innere Stadt is washed not by the Danube itself but by the Danube Canal, which acquired its present form after the major regulation of the river undertaken in the 1870s, to put an end to the periodic flooding of the city. The new bed of the Danube lies further north: the Leopoldstadt (including the Prater) and Brigittenau (including the Augarten) lie between the canal and the main river. Another arc

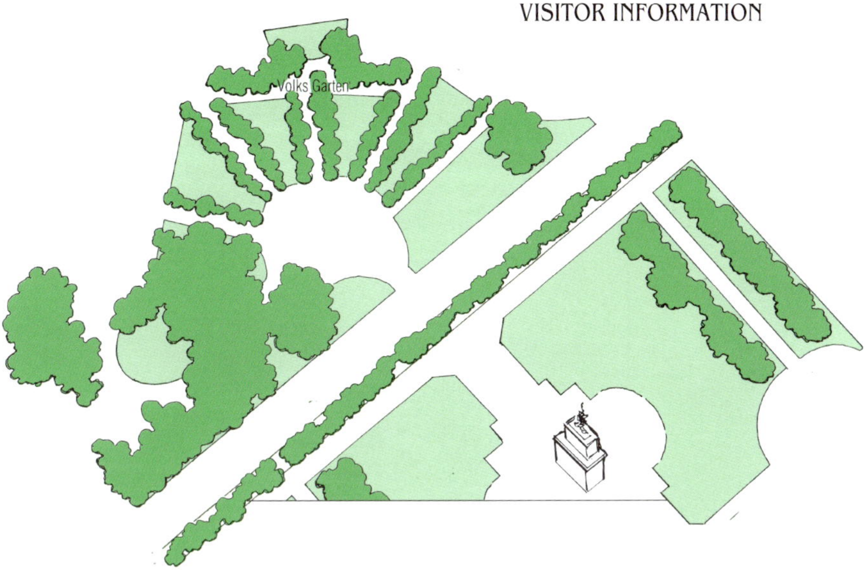

of the **Old Danube** runs through the 21st and 22nd districts and is artificially separated from the main stream. It encloses the Danube Park and UNO City (which houses international organizations such as UNIDO and the Atomic Energy Commission, and a huge modern congress centre).

You will probably do most of your sightseeing in the Innere Stadt and the districts between the Ringstrasse and the Gürtel, with the notable exception of Schönbrunn Palace which lies in the 13th district. The old Vienna of the Innere Stadt is best explored on foot, and a free gazetteer of the area can be found among the promotional literature distributed by the Tourist Board (for example in the list of hotels and pensions).

Getting around in Vienna

Public transport in the city is excellent and much preferable to using a car, especially in the Innere Stadt where street car-parking is becoming ever more problematic.

Public transport consists of an Underground (*U-Bahn*), a city transit railway (*S-Bahn*), trams (*Strassenbahn*), and buses. It is not advisable to purchase tickets for individual journeys on the trams as the machines are complicated and the tickets more expensive than if you buy them as a block (quantities of singles on a block vary) or as a season ticket. By far the best solution is to get a 24-hour travel pass (*24-Stunden-Netzkarte*), a 72-hour pass or a weekly pass (*Wochenkarte*); (the 72-hour one exists in a form giving discounts on museum entrance). Prices for these

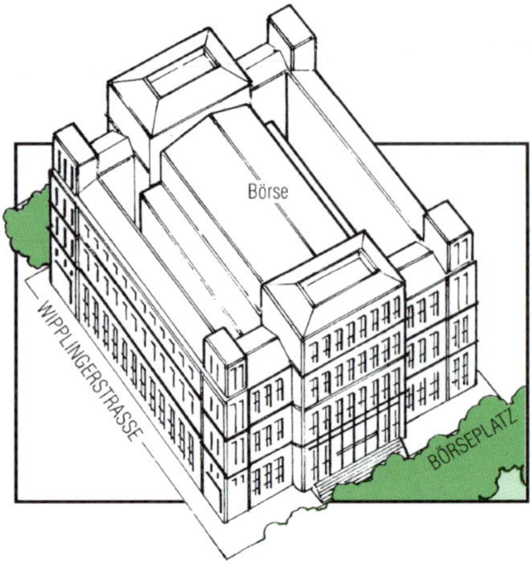

(1995) are AS50, AS130 and AS142 respectively. If you are not continuously in the city for a set period, the excursion ticket with a complicated name (*Umweltstreifennetzkarte*) at AS265 is a flexible alternative. It is a strip of eight tickets, each one valid for a whole day (24 hours). These and the single tickets from blocks (which you can buy in various quantities) are validated in machines near the doors of trams and buses, and at the entrances of U-Bahn stations. Passes and excursion tickets are valid for unlimited travel over the whole of the city centre and suburbs. Tickets may be purchased at *Tabak-Trafik* kiosks (newsagents' and tobacconists') which are found in large numbers all over the city and at transport termini.

Detailed street plans (maps such as Falk's) show the bus and tram routes and U-Bahn stations. Each tram or bus stop is clearly labelled with the route taken, but take care to check that you are heading in the direction (*Richtung*) you want. If you are heading the wrong way, the stop for the opposite direction is nearly always just across the road.

General information about public transport is available under the number 7909-105 and from offices in the pedestrian passageway at the Karlsplatz U-Bahn junction (tel. 587 31 86), at Stephansplatz U-Bahn station (tel. 512 42 27) and elsewhere, including major rail termini. Office hours are 8 am to 6 pm, weekends and holidays 8.30 am to 4 pm.

The U-Bahn

There are five lines. U1 runs north-south and over the Danube; U2 runs between Karlsplatz and Schottenring; the new U3 runs between Erdberg in the east and Johnstrasse in the west;

sions will bring it to Simmering in the east and Ottakring in the west. U4 runs from Hütteldorf in the west on a roughly semi-circular route through the city centre and back up to Heiligenstadt in the north-west; U6 runs across the western purlieus of the city from Siebenhirten to Heiligenstadt. (This line was formerly known as the *Stadtbahn*.) There is as yet no U5. Trains are clean, quiet, comfortable and regular. They operate from about 5 am until midnight.

The S-Bahn

This is used mainly by commuters coming from outlying districts. The busiest lines are the S3 in the west (out of the Westbahnhof), the S45 in the north-west (out of Heiligenstadt) and the S7 out of Praterstern/Wien Nord or Wien Mitte in the east (to the airport). The trains run between 4.30 am and midnight.

Strassenbahn

Trams run both clockwise and anti-clockwise around the Ringstrasse (it is only one way for cars), and along a dense network out of the city centre, with tentacles which reach out to the wine villages on the northern, southern and western perimeters of the city. They are somewhat slow, but ideal for sightseeing, clean and quiet. They run, depending on which line you take, generally from about 5 am until midnight.

Buses

These fill in the areas not covered by other forms of public transport, and some have routes meandering through mainly residential areas well off the beaten track. Their timetables vary, as do, in a few cases, the routes themselves (at weekends and on holidays). Between half-past midnight and 4 am night buses operate at half-hourly intervals on the main routes out of Schwedenplatz. If your route has a night bus, details will be posted on the timetable, which is fixed to the bus stop sign. On such buses you must pay a supplement – your day ticket is not valid.

Hopper buses, Nos 1A, 2A, and 3A, negotiate the narrow streets of the Innere Stadt between strategic points: Schottentor, Michaelerplatz, Graben, St. Stephan's, Schwedenplatz and Schwarzenbergplatz.

Taxis

Taxis are not officially allowed to cruise for passengers, but in practice you can often hail a taxi in the street, presumably on its way back to the rank. You will find taxi ranks at stations and at many strategic points all over the city, and also beyond the Gürtel.

Taxis summoned by telephone (extra charge of AS12) tend to come extremely promptly – and if you are still gossiping upstairs, they may well go away again. The starting price for a journey is AS24, plus about AS15 per kilometre, with a night supplement of AS10 between 11 pm and 6 am, similar supplements on Sundays. There is an extra charge for luggage.

Telephone numbers for taxis: 40100, 31300, 60160 (and many others in the phone book). If you are going to the airport, be sure to state this when you order your taxi. English is usually understood.

Private cars

It is better to leave your car outside the Ringstrasse, better still outside the Gürtel. If you must bring it into the centre, use one of the underground garages (costing about AS50 per hour) which are placed conveniently in and around the Innere Stadt, for example in front of the city hall (Rathaus), on Freyung, on Stephansplatz and beside the opera house.

Street parking in the centre during the day ranges from difficult to impossible. Areas marked by blue lines require (rather complicated) parking discs (*Parkscheiben*), obtainable from *Tabak-Trafik* kiosks, and your time is limited to one-and-a-half hours. If you are towed away, ring the police for information (313 44-92 11). It currently costs you at least AS1,700 to release your car.

There are all-night petrol stations at Morzinplatz on the Danube Canal and around the city at Neubau-Gürtel, Heiligenstädter Strasse, Hadikgasse and Triester Strasse.

Speed limits in Austria are 50 kph in towns, 100 kph on country roads and 130 kph on the *Autobahnen*. The permitted blood alcohol level for drivers is 0.8 per mille.

Viennese driving is generally graceless and aggressive. Particular care should be taken when running parallel to or crossing tram lines (trams have the right of way). If the tram stops in the middle of the road, motorists must halt behind it in order to allow passengers to cross between the pavement and the tram. Alertness is required: it is easy for the novice to overlook a tram stop where (as is quite often the case) there is no raised pavement directly beside the tram lines. The Viennese naturally assume that everyone knows the rules and tend to flood off the pavement as the tram approaches.

Useful data

Tourist information

Main tourist information offices are to be found at:

- Kärntner Strasse 38, open 9 am-7 pm;
- Schwechat Airport (in the arrivals hall), open Jun-Sep 8.30 am-11 pm, Oct-May 8.30 am-10 pm; and
- Südbahnhof, 6.30 am-10 pm.

Written requests for tourist information should be addressed to the Wiener Tourismusverband, obere Augartenstrasse 40 A-1025, Wien; Fax 216 84 92 Tel: (431 211 14-0)

All of these offices supply copious information, including extensive and detailed hotel listings. They also have a room referral service.

Sightseeing tours

Coach tours are on offer from Cityrama (departures from Stadtpark/Johannesgasse), tel. 53 413-0. Try also:

- City Touring Vienna (with hotel pick-up service), tel. 894 14 17-0;
- Stattwerkstatt, tel: 34 33 84; Kolingasse 6.
- Vienna Sightseeing Tours, Central Bus Terminal (Wien-Mitte), tel. 712 46 83-0.

Boat tours The DDSG has traditionally offered a variety of boat trips (information from Schwedenplatz 1, tel. 2181896), but the company has been battered by adverse economic winds in recent times and its future is uncertain.

Skylark In summer there are pleasure trips out of Schwechat Airport. Contact Vienna Sightseeing Tours, tel. 712 46 83-0.

Bicycling Cyclists are encouraged in Vienna with cycle routes signposted throughout the city and along the Ringstrasse. Maps of cycling routes (*Radwege*) around Vienna are available from the Information Office of the City Hall (Rathaus). General information and bicycle hire can be obtained from Vienna-Bike, tel. 319 12 58.

Other sightseeing possibilities

There is a large number of walking tours organized throughout the year, some covering the different periods of the city's architecture, some dealing with specialist themes (such as 'Sigmund

Freud and Jewish Vienna at the Turn of the Century', 'The Third Man' or 'The Viennese Coffee House'). For information, tel. 514 50-43. Note, however, that some of the commentaries may be offered in German only.

An unsual weekend attraction is the old-timer tram excursion starting from Karlsplatz, May to Sep, Sat at 1.30 pm and Sun at 11 am and 1.30 pm (tel. 98 54 553).

Guided tours of specific buildings (for instance, the Vienna International Centre, Otto Wagner's Kirche am Steinhof or the Augarten Porcelain Manufactory) are listed in the monthly programme (see Publications, page 25), as are most of the walking tours (for which see also the leaflet *Vienna Walks*).

Museums

Vienna is astonishingly rich in museums which illuminate various aspects of the Habsburg patrimony and the history of the city. Opening times are kept as complicated as possible and it is best to obtain the free leaflet *Museums Vienna* from a tourist office. The monthly listing of events features special exhibitions currently running at any museum or gallery, but even so warns that the opening times can be changed at short notice.

All museums charge an entrance fee, with the usual reductions (in most cases) for students and some other visitors. Means of identification must be shown.

Churches

Happily the Viennese require their churches to be permanently accessible, and they are therefore open during daylight hours. There are a few exceptions, however, specifically among some of the churches belonging to monastic orders, such as the Dominicans or Piarists.

Shopping, banking and business hours

Vienna shopping hours are a source of frustration to many foreign visitors and indeed to many Viennese. After a long wrangle with vested interests (consumers' views are apparently not required), an unsatisfactory half-way house now exists between the restrictive laws which used to govern opening hours and a satisfactory set of liberalized regulations. Generally, shops may open between 9 am and 6 pm on weekdays and until noon on Saturday. Food shops may open earlier and close slightly later. The new rules also allow them to stay open later on one day of the week or to open in the afternoon on the first Saturday of the month. Smaller shops outside the city centre still close over lunch, while *Tabak-Trafik* kiosks open early in the morning but close for two or three hours in the early afternoon. Only food shops and news-stands at main railway stations open long hours (until 10 or 11 pm) and also on Sunday. There is, of course, no logical reason why all shops should not open when they feel like it, but restriction suits many traders, who fear competition and higher costs, while the unions fear longer hours for their members without a fair increase in pay.

Banks are open Mon-Wed and Fri, 8 am-3 pm, on Thur until 5.30 pm. Branches outside the city centre close for lunch between 12.30 and 1.30 pm. In the spectrum of user-friendliness, or rather the lack of it, that characterizes European retail banks, the Austrians emerge with fewer minus points than most: time-wasting is kept to a minimum and clerks are helpful. There are exchange bureaux with non-banking hours at the airport, the City Air Terminal, the Westbahnhof, the Südbahnhof and in the Opera Passage. Exchange automats accepting some western currencies (including Sterling) are located along Kärntner Strasse and on Stephansplatz.

Public holidays

The following public holidays are observed in Vienna: New Year's Day (1 January); Three Kings (6 January); Easter Monday; 1 May; Ascension Day; Whit Monday; Corpus Christi (2 June); Assumption of Mary (15 August); National Day (26 October); All Saints (1 November) Conception of Mary (8 December); Christmas (25, 26 December).

In addition, shortened hours and closures may be anticipated on Good Friday, All Souls (2 November), Christmas Eve and 31 December.

Restaurants

All-day eating is possible in Vienna's many cafés, and also in self-service chains such as Naschmarkt and Nordsee, although hot meals (*warme Küche*) may be restricted to lunch and supper hours. Otherwise, restaurant opening times are largely what you might expect, but beware some gourmet places that close rather early (such as the excellent Hedrich at Stubenring 2, which closes at 9 pm and all weekend). From about 7 pm the bars, discos and night-spots within the so-called 'Bermuda Triangle' in the north-western part of the Innere Stadt begin to come to life.

A complete listing of all eating establishments, categorized by district and type, is to be found in *Wien wie es ißt...*, available in bookshops and updated annually. Gourmets consult the *Gault Millau* for Austria, or *Österreich A la Carte*, both of which are easy to find, although their combination of peacock prose with unfair nit-picking irritates some readers.

The Post

Post offices open Mon-Fri between 8 am and noon, and 2 pm to 6 pm. The main post office, Fleischmarkt 19, tel. 515 090, is open around the clock, as are the offices at the Westbahnhof and the Südbahnhof.

Telephones

Telephone and telegram facilities exist in all post offices. Off the Kohlmarkt, in Wallnerstrasse, and off Stephansplatz there are automatic international telephones which accept credit cards. Otherwise telephone cards of various values can be bought at *Tabak-Trafik* kiosks and post offices, and are the most convenient method of paying for a call from a public telephone.

For international calls dial 00, then the country code followed by the city/area code and the number, but omitting the 0 prefix (for example, London numbers dialled from Vienna are either 0044171 or 0044181). For the U.S.A. and Canada the country code is 1, for the U.K. 44. To call Germany dial 060, and Switzerland 050, then the city code (omitting the 0 prefix). The city code for Vienna is 0222 if dialled from within Austria, or 1 if dialled from abroad. The international code for Austria is 43.

Directory enquiries is 1611 (for numbers in Austria) and 1612 for Germany, 1613 for other European countries and 1614 for countries outside Europe. For telegrams dial 190.

The preliminary pages of telephone directories give complete listings of service numbers and all domestic and foreign codes, together with those of selected towns abroad to which direct dial is possible.

Vienna for children

A visit to Schönbrunn could include the zoo (Tiergarten) at the western end of the park, which is open daily from 9 am until dusk or 6 pm, whichever is the sooner. The *Schloss* and park generally contain a number of sights that would appeal to children, such as the huge palm house and the carriage museum.

The Technisches Museum für Industrie und Gewerbe (Technology Museum), Mariahilfer Strasse 212, is not far away and is full of such things as early steam engines, rolling-stock, aeroplanes, automobiles, industrial machines and so on. However, it is currently under renovation, so check in advance whether it has reopened, tel. 914 16 10-0. Other museums that might be of interest to children include:

• The Natural History Museum, Maria Theresien-Platz;
• The Theatre Museum, newly-installed in the Palais Lobkowitz on Lobkowitzplatz.

For teenagers, Jugendinformation Wien provides information on cultural events and sporting activities of interest to young people. It is located in the Bellaria Passage under the tram stop at Dr.-Karl-Renner-Ring, tel. 526 4637, Mon-Fri 12 noon to 7 pm, Sat 10 am-7 pm.

If you read German, it is worth buying the paperback *Kind in Wien* (Falter Verlag).

A babysitting service is available; tel. 523 39 24.

Publications

The absolutely indispensable accompaniment to a Viennese holiday is the monthly *Programm* (listing of events), obtainable free from tourist offices. This gives details of virtually every concert, operatic and theatrical performance, lecture, exhibition and other event or show taking place that month, together with venues, starting times and booking arrangements.

For a list of sights the *Vienna A to Z* (published by the Tourist Board and available at *Tabak-Trafik* kiosks and elsewhere), is well worth its modest cover price.

Foreign embassies and consulates

• **Australia** Mattiellistrasse 2-4, 4th district; tel. 512 737 10.
• **Canada** Schubertring 10-12, 1st district; tel. 533 36 91.
• **Germany** Metternichgasse 3, 3rd district; tel. 711 54.
• **Ireland** in the Hilton Hotel (16th floor), Landstrasser Hauptstrasse 2, 3rd district; tel. 715 42 46.
• **New Zealand** Springsiedelgasse 28; tel, 318 8505.
• **South Africa** Sandgasse 33, 19th district; tel. 32 64 93.
• **Switzerland** Prinz-Eugen-Strasse 7, 3rd district; tel. 795 05-0.
• **United Kingdom** Jaurësgasse 12, 3rd district; tel. 714 61 17(consular section).

• **U.S.A.** (consular section) in the Marriott Hotel, Gartenbaupromenade 2, Parkring 12a, 1st district; tel. 313 39.

Emergencies

Emergency telephone numbers

• Fire dial 122.
• Police dial 133.
• Doctor (only in emergency) dial 141.
• Dentist (information out of hours) tel. 512 20 78.
• Ambulance dial 144.
• Befrienders (English speaking) dial 713 3374.

Casualty

Allgemeines Krankenhaus der Stadt Wien, Alser Strasse 4; tel. 40 400.

Pharmacies

Pharmacies are generally open Mon-Fri 8 am to noon, and 2 pm to 6 pm; Sat 8 am to noon.

For a taped list of pharmacists on call out of hours, dial 1550. An extra fee will be charged for rousing pharmacists outside working hours.

For those without health insurance or money the splendid *Barmherzigen Brüder*, Grosse Mohrengasse 9, in the 2nd district, tel. 211 21-0, will provide emergency help.

Car breakdowns

There are two automobile clubs with emergency numbers: ARBÖ, dial 123, and öAMTC, dial 120. It is worth your while to check whether your club is affiliated to either of these before you leave.

Lost property

Try the office in the Wasagasse 22, in the 9th district, tel. 31 34 40. Hours are Mon-Fri 8 am to 1pm. Railway lost property: Langauergasse 2; tel. 580 00. Open Mon–Fri 8 am to 3.30 pm.

U-Bahn map

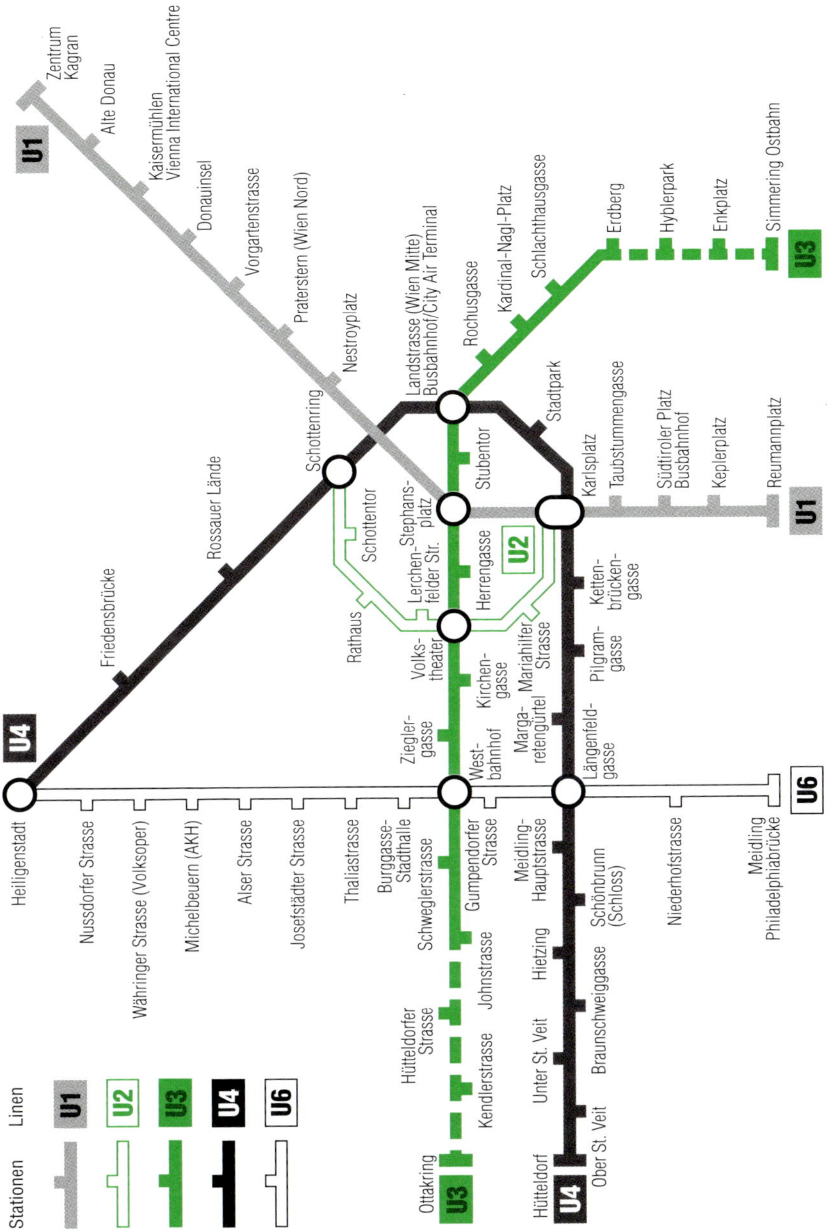

Stationen
Linen
U1
U2
U3
U4
U6
Zentrum Kagran
Alte Donau
Kaisermühlen Vienna International Centre
Donauinsel
Vorgartenstrasse
Praterstern (Wien Nord)
Nestroyplatz
Schottenring
Landstrasse (Wien Mitte) Busbahnhof/City Air Terminal
Rochusgasse
Kardinal-Nagl-Platz
Schlachthausgasse
Erdberg
Hyblerpark
Enkplatz
Simmering Ostbahn
Stadtpark
Stubentor
Stephans-platz
Karlsplatz
Taubstummengasse
Südtiroler Platz Busbahnhof
Keplerplatz
Reumannplatz
Rossauer Lände
Friedensbrücke
Schottentor
Rathaus
Lerchen-felder Str.
Herrengasse
Volks-theater
Kirchen-gasse
Mariahilfer Strasse
Ketten-brücken-gasse
Pilgram-gasse
Marga-retengürtel
Längenfeld-gasse
Ziegler-gasse
West-bahnhof
Heiligenstadt
Nussdorfer Strasse
Währinger Strasse (Volksoper)
Michelbeuern (AKH)
Alser Strasse
Josefstädter Strasse
Thaliastrasse
Burggasse-Stadthalle
Schweglerstrasse
Gumpendorfer Strasse
Meidling-Hauptstrasse
Schönbrunn (Schloss)
Niederhofstrasse
Meidling Philadelphiabrücke
Johnstrasse
Hietzing
Braunschweiggasse
Hütteldorfer Strasse
Kendlerstrasse
Unter St. Veit
Ober St. Veit
Ottakring
Hütteldorf

Master location map

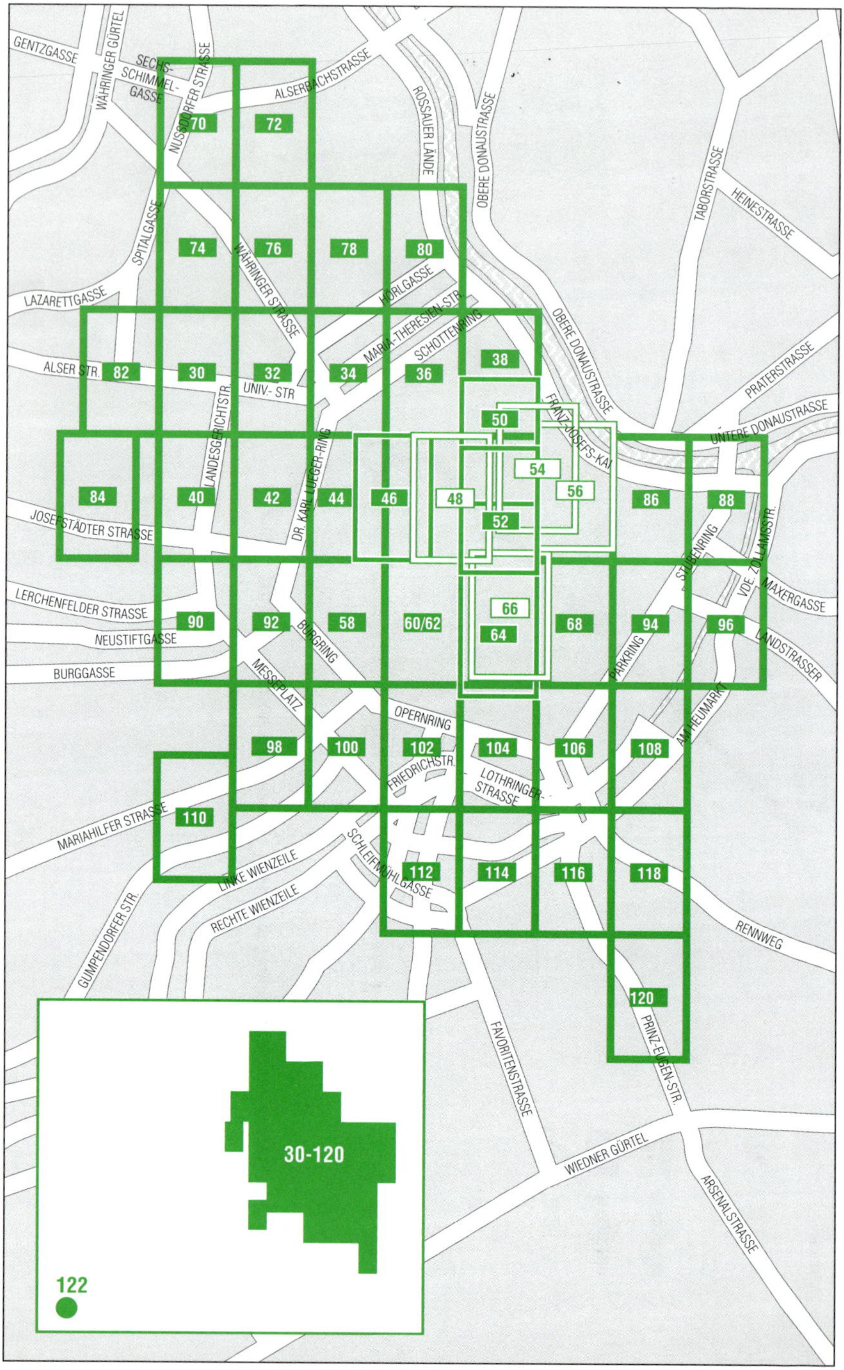

THE MAPS

▲ 74

1
GRÜNFELDGASSE
FRANKGASSE
OTTO-WAGNER-PLATZ
HAULERSTRASSE
ALSER STRASSE
FRANKH
2
Landesgericht für Strafsachen Wien
3
SCHLÖSSELGASSE
WICKENBURGGASSE
Arbeitsgericht Wien
LANDESGERICHTSSTRASSE
GRILLPARZERSTRAS
FLORIANIGASSE
4
TULPENGASSE

▼ 40

① The imposing **Österreichische Nationalbank** (Austrian National Bank) (off map) at Otto-Wagner-Platz 3 was built by a pupil of Wagner named Leopold Bauer. When he started work on it in 1913, it was still the Austro-Hungarian Bank, acquiring its present name after the collapse of the Dual Monarchy (1918). The National Bank has considerable independence and is charged with protecting the value of the currency, a task it has managed with conspicuous success over the years. However, much indignation has recently been aroused by the revelation that its chief executive receives a salary half as much again as that of the Chairman of the Federal Reserve in America; it also transpired that substantial salaries were being drawn by personnel whose contribution to the work of the bank was all but invisible. The lingering elements of a semi-corporate state in Austria's system of government have produced a number of such anomalies, gravy trains well shielded from the vulgar gaze of the public. From the end of the Second World War until 1955 the American occupation force had its headquarters in the National Bank building. On Frankhplatz nearby is a monument of Indiana limestone marking the boundary of the American zone as it existed between 1945 and 1955. ② The neo-Classical **Landesgericht** (Provincial Court) at Landesgerichtstrasse 11 is popularly known as the *graue Haus* (grey house) and is indeed a lowering sort of building that has been many times enlarged. It was custom-built for the court in 1839 by Johann Fischer and also contained a prison (the first inmates were crooked contractors who had skimped on the building). A plaque on the wall records that Austrian resistance fighters were executed here between 1938 and 1945. To the west of the court, between Wickenburggasse and Schlösselgasse is ③ one of the interwar *Gemeindebauten* (social housing blocks), the **Terese-Schlesinger-Hof**, designed by Caesar Poppovits and named after a Social Democratic M.P. It was built on the site of the Riedhof, one of Vienna's most famous 19thC restaurants: regular patrons included the surgeon Billroth, the composer Anton Bruckner and the Liberal Mayor, Cajetan Felder. ④ At **Schlösselgasse No. 7** Emanuel Schikaneder, the impresario and librettist for *The Magic Flute*, died in poverty on 21 September 1812. Of the opera, he is said to have complained that he had written a wonderful text, "but that fellow Mozart ruined it all with his music".

▲ 76

FRANKGASSE
GARNISONGASSE
WÄHRINGER STRASSE
ROOSEVELTPLATZ
1
Votivkirche
2
Sigmund Freud
UNIVERSITÄTSSTRASSE
3
RATHAUSSTRASSE
LIEBIGGASSE
EBENDORFESTRASSE
REICHSRATSSTRASSE
Universitäten Wien
GRILLPARZERSTRASSE
RATHAUSPLATZ
FELDERSTRASSE

▼ 42

Rooseveltplatz, a park receding from the busy traffic junction of Schottentor, is dominated by ① the **Votivkirche**, the ambitious neo-Gothic church built between 1856 and 1879. Progress was slow because the 27-year-old architect, Heinrich Ferstel, insisted on the best materials, hand-worked by expert craftsmen, so that the church should as nearly as possible replicate a medieval building. The impulse for building the church was provided by Franz Joseph's survival of an assassination attempt while taking his midday constitutional on the bastions. His brother Maximilian (later the ill-fated Emperor of Mexico) suggested building a church in thanksgiving for the narrow escape. Ferstel (whose relief portrait can be seen over the chancel) won the commission against formidable local and international competition. His design drew inspiration from French and German Gothic cathedrals that he had studied on his travels. Objects of interest in the church include the tomb of Count Salm, commander of Vienna's defence in the first Turkish siege in 1529. Bordering the square is the university. Students gather in ② the **Café Maximilian** opposite at Universitätsstrasse 2 (**S**). Maximilian was executed 12 years before the consecration of the votive church whose moving spirit he had been, but the square in front of it retained his name until the end of the Dual Monarchy. The coffee-house was opened around the turn of the century. It has a sun-terrace on the park side and offers typical Viennese fare from 7 am to midnight. On the other side of the street at No. 7 is ③ the ugly **Neue Institutsgebäude** of the University (1962) erected on the site of the *Generalkommandogebäude* (Headquarters of the Chiefs of Staff) which had been bombed in the Second World War. ④ The **New University** (superseding the original Baroque one on Ignaz Seipel Platz, *see page 87*) was built at No. 1 Dr.-Karl-Lueger-Ring in 1884. The architect was again Heinrich Ferstel. This time he adopted the style of the Italian Renaissance, a reminder of the cradle of modern European culture. In the internal courtyards are various monuments to educationalists, notable among them Maria Theresa's two enlightened ministers, Joseph von Sonnenfels (scion of a family of converted Jews) and Gerhard van Swieten (a Dutchman; *see pages 74-75*). Sonnenfels, as chief censor, considerably relaxed the stifling suppression of ideas which had taken place under absolutism.

▲ 78

▲ 32

HÖRLGASSE
WASAGASSE
LIECHTENSTEINSTRASSE
PEREGRINGASSE
KOLINGASSE
Hst. Schottentor
5
6
WÄHRINGER STRASSE
MARIA-THERESIEN-STRASSE
4
Sigmund Freud Park
SCHOTTENRING
Hst. Schottentor
HESSGASSE
2
SCHOTTENBASTEI
1
HELFERSTORFERSTRASSE
DR.-KARL-LUEGER-RING
SCHOTTENGASSE
3
MÖLKER BASTEI
MÖLKER STEIG

▼ 44

Schottentor, at the south-western corner of the Ringstrasse, is a major tram junction, with stations at street level and below ground level (the latter constructed in 1961). From here trams leave for the western purlieus of the city and for the villages on the edge of the Wienerwald, such as Grinzing and Nussdorf. On the edge of Schottentor at Dr.-Karl-Lueger-Ring 14 is ① the **Ephrussi Palais** built by Theophil Hansen. The sumptuous palace was built for a banker and is now owned by Casinos Austria. To the north, opposite the junction, is ② the huge and splendid main office of the **Creditanstalt Bankverein** (Schottengasse 6-8). ③ At Schottengasse 7 is a later **historicist house** with bay windows and little towers designed by Fellner and Hellmer, a firm that built theatres all over the Austro-Hungarian Empire. The ground floor restaurant **Kupferdachl** (**Zum Leupold**) (**SSS**) is excellent. Across Schottenring at No. 3 is ④ the **Hotel de France** (**SS-SSS**), with an attractive café and a cinema that shows films in English. Post-Modern, but with an allusive nod or two in the direction of the Vienna Secession, is ⑤ the **Hilton-Plaza Hotel** at No. 11 (**SSS**). Originally the Hotel Austria was erected on this site for the World Exhibition of 1873. In the 1980s the new establishment was built to Kurt Hlawenicka's elegant design, the front of the building being faced with marble cladding, and enlivened by decorative highlighting in brown and gold. Between the two hotels is ⑥ the **Polizei Direktion** (7-9 Schottenring). It was put up in 1974 and occupies the site where the Ringtheater once stood. The theatre burned down with considerable loss of life before a performance on 8 December 1881. The composer Anton Bruckner (who lived in a flat next door at Schottenring 5) was so appalled by what he saw that he refused to have any naked light in his dwelling thereafter. The cause of the catastrophe was gas lighting that failed to ignite so that gas streamed into the auditorium, bursting into flame when the lamps were finally alight. Four hundred people died, mostly of asphyxiation, and Richard Wagner expressed the hope that plenty of Jews were among them (as was indeed the case). In 1885 Franz Joseph ordered a *Sühnhaus* (House of Atonement) to be built where the theatre had stood; the architect was Friedrich von Schmidt (who built the City Hall). Profits from the rent of its apartments were to be used for charitable purposes. The parents of the first child to be born in the new house happened to be Sigmund and Martha Freud. They were gratified to receive a personal message of congratulation from the Emperor and a gift of flowers.

▲ 80

▲ 34

MARIA-THERESIEN-STRASSE
SCHOTTENRING
BÖRSEGASSE
NEUTORGASSE
ZELINKAGASSE
ESSLINGGASSE
1
Börse
WIPPLINGERSTRASSE
BÖRSEPLATZ
BÖRSEPLATZ
WERDERTORGASSE
HOHENSTAUFENGASSE
2
HELFERSTORFERSTRASSE
3
ROCKHGASSE
RENNGASSE
4
5
TIEFER GRABEN
RENNGASSE

▼ 46 ▼ 48

① The **Börse** (Stock Exchange) at Schottenring 16 is one of Theophil Hansen's loveliest buildings. The neo-Renaissance exterior positively glows with elegance, much of the effect achieved by the combination of cool white stone for architectural furniture with warm red brick from the Wienerberg for the fabric. The leitmotif of the sculptural decoration is Poseidon, chosen for the implicit associations of trade with seafaring. The building is no less attractive inside with a noble vestibule, overlooked by a visitors' gallery and two ceremonial stairways flanked by columns of yellow, red and black marble. Hansen, who thought of everything, even had under-floor heating installed. The Börse had occupied no less than three different homes after its foundation by Maria Theresa in 1771, before finally becoming established here. It is a small market and the institutions (especially banks) have large block and cross holdings which makes it relatively unattractive for the small investor. The immediate vicinity of the Börse has only recently been declared a conservation area, and that is no doubt the reason why ② a decidedly *outré* building could be built here as late as 1983. This is the **Juridicum** (Faculty of Jurisprudence of the University of Vienna) at Helferstorferstrasse 9-15, designed by Ernst Hiesmayr. It has a rather top-heavy look about it, but also a number of interesting features including liquid-filled columns. Two modern sculptures – *Meditation Stone* and *Gogarte Rancate* stand at either side of the building. Nearby at Hohenstaufengasse 9 is ③ a **house** with a classical frieze on the façade – the home of archaeologist Alois Hauser, who designed it in collaboration with his brother. In neighbouring Rockhgasse at No. 4 is ④ the **Giro und Cassenverein bank** designed by Emil von Förster, architect of the ill-fated Ringtheater (*see page 35*). It has now been converted into classy apartments. Walking east along Wipplingerstrasse one soon comes to ⑤ the **Hohe Brücke** (High Bridge) over the Tiefen Graben. This turn-of-the-century iron construction was built by Josef Hackhofer and Karl Christl. The original lampstands remain. From the 15thC there had been a stone bridge here, and in the 18thC a statue of John Nepomuk was introduced, the protection of the saint evidently being thought desirable. Panels on the side of the iron bridge depict its predecessors, but they can only be seen from below. A plaque on a house at the east end recalls that one of the city gates was situated here in Babenberg times (the Babenbergs were predecessors of the Habsburgs).

Hst. Schottenring
DONAUKANAL
FRANZ-JOSEFS-KAI
ZELINKAGASSE
GONZAGAGASSE
ESSLINGGASSE
WERDERTORGASSE
NEUTORGASSE
HEINRICHSGASSE
RUDOLFSPLATZ
GÖLSDORFGASSE
CONCORDIAPLATZ
BÖRSEGASSE
MARIENSTIEGE
1
SALZGRIES
GONZAGAGASSE
AM GESTADE
2
4
PASSAUER PLATZ
3
SCHWERTGASSE
FISCHERSTIEGE
SALZTORGASSE
SALVATORGASSE
VORLAUFSTRASSE

▲ 36

▼ 50/52

The strip of land along the Danube Canal from the Rossauer Lände up to the raised promontory of Maria am Gestade was once dotted with communities of fishermen and others who made their living from the river. ① The **Salzgries** (formerly *An dem Gries* – a reference to the muddy shore) was a docking area even in Roman times. After 1322 it was known as Salzgries because imported salt was unloaded at this point. Then it was a street full of taverns and cheap lodgings for boatmen. In 1748 a huge barracks was built along most of the north side, in anticipation of a Franco-Prussian attack on Vienna. It remained until 1880, when the present houses replaced it. Below the steep steps to the church of Maria am Gestade you will pass ② a sculptural group which is known as the **Hannakenbrunnen**. Rudolf Schmidt's and Hubert Matuschek's modern fountain (1937) recalls the legend of a Moravian doctor living in the vicinity, who hit upon a novel way of increasing his income: night-time passers-by were beaten up by his servants, after which the doctor himself appeared from the shadows to dress the victims' wounds for a substantial fee. You reach Passauer Platz via the steps to the church. At No. 6 ③ the **court and administration of the Passau bishops** stood for several centuries; all of it except for a small convent was demolished in 1822. Vienna belonged to the Passau diocese until 1469, when it acquired its own bishop. The *Hof* was the scene of important negotiations between the overmighty bishops of Passau and the town's representatives, who were continually striving for autonomy. Later, Protestants and Anabaptists were imprisoned in the building. Nearby, at Schwertgasse 3, is a remarkable Baroque portal of 1720, and above it a fine Pietà. Adalbert Stifter, who wrote one of the classic novels of the Biedermeier period, lived here for a short while in the 1830s. **Maria am Gestade** (St Mary on the Bank) ④ is one of the loveliest Gothic churches in Vienna. Built by Michael Knab in 1330 on a narrow site above the river (then lapping at the banks immediately below), it has a noticeable misalignment between nave and chancel. Its open-work filigree tower is a landmark, appearing in the earliest city views by Gothic painters. The exterior is a fine example of late Gothic, but much of the interior's trappings are 19thC additions. Inside, you can see the tomb of Clemens Maria Hofbauer, a celebrated Moravian preacher in the late 18th and early 19thC. In 1914 Hofbauer was declared Patron Saint of the city.

▲ 30

TULPENGASSE
Floriani Park
SCHMIDGASSE
FRIEDRICH-SCHMIDT-PLATZ
Rathaus
6
LENAUGASSE
6
BUCHFELDGASSE
Hst. Rathaus
LANDESGERICHTSSTRASSE
JOSEFSTADTER STRASSE
4
RATHAUSSTRASSE
LICHTEN
STADIONGASSE
3
JOSEFSGASSE
DOBLHOFFGASSE
BARTENSTEING
AUERSPERGSTRASSE
5
1
2

▼ 90

Auerspergstrasse/Landesgerichtsstrasse

① The elegant **Auersperg-Palais** at Auerspergstrasse 1 (off map) has been considerably altered from Lukas von Hildebrandt's original design of 1706. Johann Neupauer remodelled the middle part in 1722 and the neo-Classical interior is the work of Heinrich Fischer (1802). The façade was again altered when the street level was raised in the late 19thC. A plaque on the wall reads as follows: 'In 1945 Austrian patriots meeting in this house prevented the destruction of Vienna and laid the foundations for a free Austria. In memory of those who gave their lives for the resistance movement.' Between 1945 and 1955 the palace was the headquarters of the military police of the four occupying powers (the Russians, Americans, French and British). In 1954 it was renovated and since then spring balls, exhibitions and various other events take place here. ② One of the many lodgings of Beethoven (he is said to have moved 80 times during his 36-year sojourn in Vienna) is to be found at **Auerspergstrasse 3/Trautsongasse 2** (off map). Here he composed the beautiful 'Credo' of the *Missa Solemnis*. The house (1796) has decorative terracotta reliefs on the façade. At the Trautsongasse entrance are plaster copies of Raphael Donner's *Judgement of Paris* and *Vulcan's Forge* (originals in the Lower Belvedere), together with an oil painting of the house as it was in the 18thC. ③ The neo-Baroque building at Josefsgasse 12 is **Vienna's English Theatre**. After the war it was for a while the Nestroy Theatre, but in 1972 the English Theatre (founded in 1962 by Ruth Brinkmann and Franz Schafranek) took the place over. The performances, all in English, are of a high standard and quite well known guest stars regularly appear. ④ The **Café Rathaus** at Landesgerichtsstrasse 5 is a traditional 145-year old Viennese café with card-playing and chess, as well as a TV room (**S**). There is a small summer garden (open 8 am to midnight). ⑤ The **Rathauskeller** (Felderstrasse/Rathausplatz 1, **SS** used for tour groups) (off map) is leased by the City of Vienna. The heavily ornate interior (1899) is decorated with Historicist frescoes, scenes from the Viennese past, coats of arms of the Austrian Crown Lands and the like. ⑥ **Buchfeldgasse** occupies the area that was once the estate of Marchese Malaspina. It has retained its attractive Biedermeier façades (the houses were all built between 1824 and 1828). In the **Lenaugasse** that runs parallel to Buchfeldgasse there are similarly attractive 18th and 19thC dwellings.

▲ 32

FELDERSTRASSE
EBENDORFERSTRASSE
RATHAUSPLATZ
RATHAUSPLATZ
Rathauspark
1
Rathaus
RATHAUSPLATZ
2
DR. KARL-RENNER-RING
LICHTENFELSGASSE
3
Rathauspark
BARTENSTEINGASSE
STADIONGASSE
RATHAUSPLATZ
4
Parlament
REICHSRATSSTRASSE
DOBLHOFFGASSE

▼ 92

① The **Rathaus** (City Hall) is one of Vienna's great landmarks, an enormously ambitious display of architectural Historicism created by Friedrich von Schmidt between 1872 and 1883, and conceived as the incarnation of civic pride. It encompasses seven inner courtyards, numerous stairways, loggias, arcades, balconies, vestibules, offices and reception rooms. Highlights are the magnificent **Festsaal** and the **Council Chamber** itself, with its coffered ceiling, elegant gallery for visitors and frescoed vaults by Ludwig Meyer. The City Library and the Archive of the City and Province of Vienna are also situated in the Rathaus. The acres of neo-Gothic façade are no less impressive than the interior. On the three sides of the projecting central tower are equestrian reliefs of the Emperor Franz Joseph, Rudolf of Habsburg (the first of the dynasty to rule in Austria) and Rudolf IV, 'the Founder', who did more to elevate the status of Vienna than almost any other Habsburg. Atop the 98-m high tower itself is a banner-carrying knight, the **Rathausmann**, made from just over 1.8 tonnes of copper by Alexander Nehr. The model for it was the representation of Maximilian I (1459-1519) kept in the armoury of the Neue Burg. ② The **Rathausplatz and Park** in front of the City Hall is also a pantheon to great historical personalities associated with Vienna. One of the most arresting is Alfred Hrdlicka's representation (1967) of Karl Renner, first president of Austria. Tours of the Rathaus interior take place Mon-Fri at 1 pm. Concerts are held in the arcades and in the park during the Wiener Festwochen (Vienna Festival Weeks) and for three weeks before Christmas the Christkindlmarkt (Christmas Market) is held here, a brash and lively fair with assorted booths and entertainments. At Rathausplatz 8 under the arcades is ③ the **Konditorei Sluka**, much favoured by the local bureaucrats and M.P.s. The cakes and pastries are their own production and a light lunch is available – at a price. It is open Mon-Fri, 8 am-7 pm (**S**). ④ **Parlament** (Houses of Parliament, 1883) at Dr.-Karl-Renner-Ring was until 1918 the Reichsratsgebäude (the Parliament of the Austro-Hungarian Empire). Theophil Hansen built it in severe classical style, a reference to democracy's birth in Ancient Greece. The Federal Parliament has two houses, the Nationalrat and the Bundesrat; the former is elected for a four-year term by proportional representation and has 183 members. The latter has 63 members sent by the Austrian States. Guided tours of the interior (if Parliament is not sitting) take place Mon-Fri at 11 am; in Jul and Aug also at 10 am, 1 pm and 2 pm.

▲ 34

▲ 42

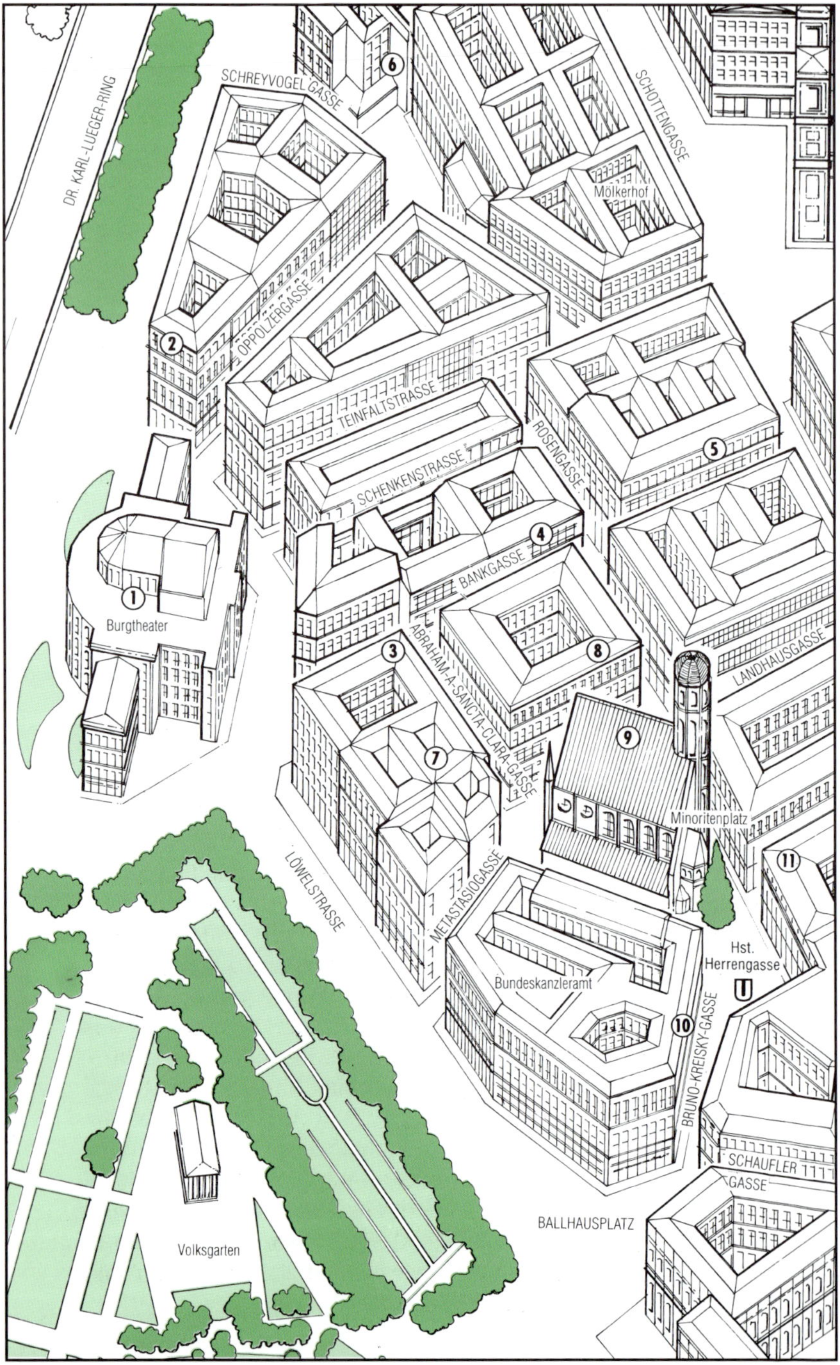
DR. KARL-LUEGER-RING
SCHREYVOGELGASSE
SCHOTTENGASSE
Mölkerhof
OPPOLZERGASSE
TEINFALTSTRASSE
SCHENKENSTRASSE
ROSENGASSE
BANKGASSE
Burgtheater
ABRAHAM-A-SANCTA-CLARA-GASSE
LANDHAUSGASSE
Minoritenplatz
LÖWELSTRASSE
METASTASIOGASSE
Bundeskanzleramt
Hst.
Herrengasse
U
BRUNO-KREISKY-GASSE
SCHAUFLER GASSE
BALLHAUSPLATZ
Volksgarten
1
2
3
4
5
6
7
8
9
10
11

▲ 40

▼ 58

① The **Burgtheater** (1888) at Dr.-Karl-Lueger-Ring 2 replaced the old Hofburgtheater on the Michaelerplatz that had originally been founded by Maria Theresa in 1741. The ceilings of the stairways in both the lateral wings of the theatre have frescoes depicting the development of drama from earliest times. The Burgtheater attracted satirical comment at first, because of its technical imperfections. The saying went that "in Parliament you can't hear the proceedings, in the City Hall you can't see them, and in the Burgtheater you can neither see nor hear anything at all". Alterations to improve the auditorium were undertaken in due course by the architect Emil von Förster. Guided tours are possible; for information tel. 514 44, extension 2182. ② **Café Landtmann** at Dr.-Karl-Lueger-Ring 4 is one of the great Ringstrassen cafés (**S**, founded in 1873). It is traditionally the haunt of literati, actors, politicians and academics. (Open daily 8 am to midnight). On the edge of Bankgasse behind the theatre is ③ the **Liechtenstein Majoratshaus**, the Viennese seat of the Liechtensteins, a Baroque palace designed by Domenico Martinelli. Further along Bankgasse at ④ Nos 4-6 is the **Hungarian Embassy**, two Baroque palaces knocked together by Franz Hillebrand in 1784. Beyond that is ⑤ the **Batthyány-Palais** with a striking façade after Fischer von Erlach. Further north at Schreyvogelgasse 10 is ⑥ the charming little **Dreimäderlhaus**, a middle-class dwelling of 1803 that is one of the best-preserved examples of neo-Classical domestic architecture to have survived. ⑦ No. 3 Minoritenplatz is the **Dietrichstein-Palais** (1755) by Franz Hillebrand with attractive rococo portals. At No. 5 is ⑧ the **Starhemberg-Palais**, which now houses the Ministry of Education. ⑨ The Gothic **Minoritenkirche** (1380) dominates the square; the architect was a monk named James of Paris. Note the fine reliefs over the west door (*The Crucifixion, Madonna and Child, St Francis Receiving the Stigmata*). The rather bleak interior is not enhanced by a tasteless mosaic copy of Leonardo's *Last Supper* by Giacomo Raffaelli. It was commissioned by Napoleon. ⑩ The **Bundeskanzleramt** (Chancellor's office) at Ballhausplatz 2 was built by Lukas von Hildebrandt and altered by Nikolaus Pacassi in 1766. Metternich held negotiations here during the Congress of Vienna (1814-15). Chancellor Dollfuss was murdered in one of its rooms during the attempted Nazi putsch of 25 July 1934. ⑪ The new **Bundesamtsgebäude** (Ballhausplatz 3/Minoritenplatz 9) is a rather impressive piece of modern architecture, built between 1982 and 1986 by Machart, Moebius and Partners.

▲ 34
▲ 36
▲ 44

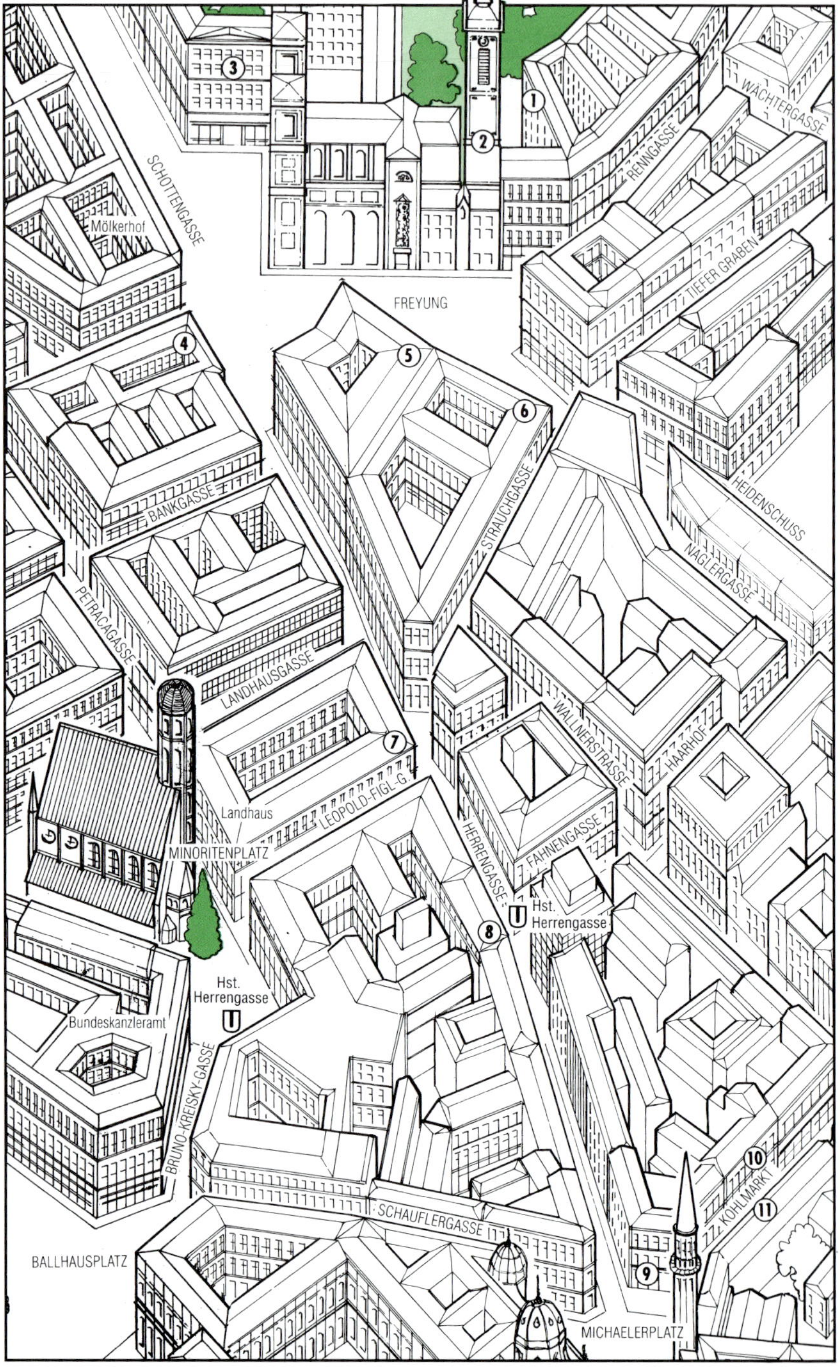

▼ 58
▼ 60/62

The name *Freyung* denotes the freedom from arrest granted in medieval times to miscreants on the run who made it to ① the **Schottenstift** on the north side of the square. The 'Scottish Cloister' was actually founded around 1155 by Irish monks (Ireland was known as 'Scotia Maior'). Incorporated in the cloister is ② the somewhat gloomy **church**, originally Gothic but later altered to Baroque. Its most famous works of art are the 19 painted panels by the 'Schottenmeister' (1475), now displayed in the adjacent Prelacy Museum in the ③ Schottenhof. ④ The **Kinsky Palais** at Freyung 4 (off map) is one of the most elegant buildings by Lukas von Hildebrandt. The ornamental staircase inside (unfortunately not usually accessible) is an example of Baroque architecture at its most refined. ⑤ is the vast **Harrach-Palais** by Domenico Martinelli (1702); restoration has just been completed by the new owners, the Creditanstalt Bankverein. Adjoining the Harrach Palais on the Herrengasse side is ⑥ the so-called **Ferstel-Palais**, named after its architect, Heinrich Ferstel, and originally planned as a complex to include the Austro-Hungarian Bank and the Stock Exchange. The complex of buildings includes the **Café Central**, an elegant and expensive coffee-house (**SS**). The predecessor of the present café was one of the most famous hang-outs of the literati at the turn of the century. It was here that the young but already feared satirist, Karl Kraus, got his ears boxed by the outraged victims of one of his most merciless demolition jobs. At ⑦ No. 13 Herrengasse you come to the **Diet for Lower Austria**. The 1848 revolution began here with inflammatory speeches by the delegates. At Herrengasse 9 is ⑧ the **Lower Austria Museum**, in the courtyard of which is a well with a fine wrought-iron cover dating to 1570. ⑨ is the controversial **Loos-Haus** built for the tailors Goldman and Salatsch by Adolf Loos in 1912. It now belongs to a bank and has been beautifully restored. In the Kohlmarkt, one of the most ancient streets of Vienna, you find ⑩ the famous **Demel Konditorei**, founded in 1786 (**S**). Despite the discomfort of the box-like rooms and the high prices, visitors flock for Demel's famous confections. The place acquired a touch of notoriety in the 1970s when it was owned by Austria's most spectacular con-man, Udo Proksch, now in prison: he invited corruptible persons of influence to his Club 45 in an upstairs room for 'discussions'. The café is open 10 am-8 pm. On the opposite side of the street Demel has opened a smart diner ⑪ called **Demel Vis-à-Vis** which is open from 11 am to 7 pm (**SS**).

▲ 36 ▲ 38

▲ 46

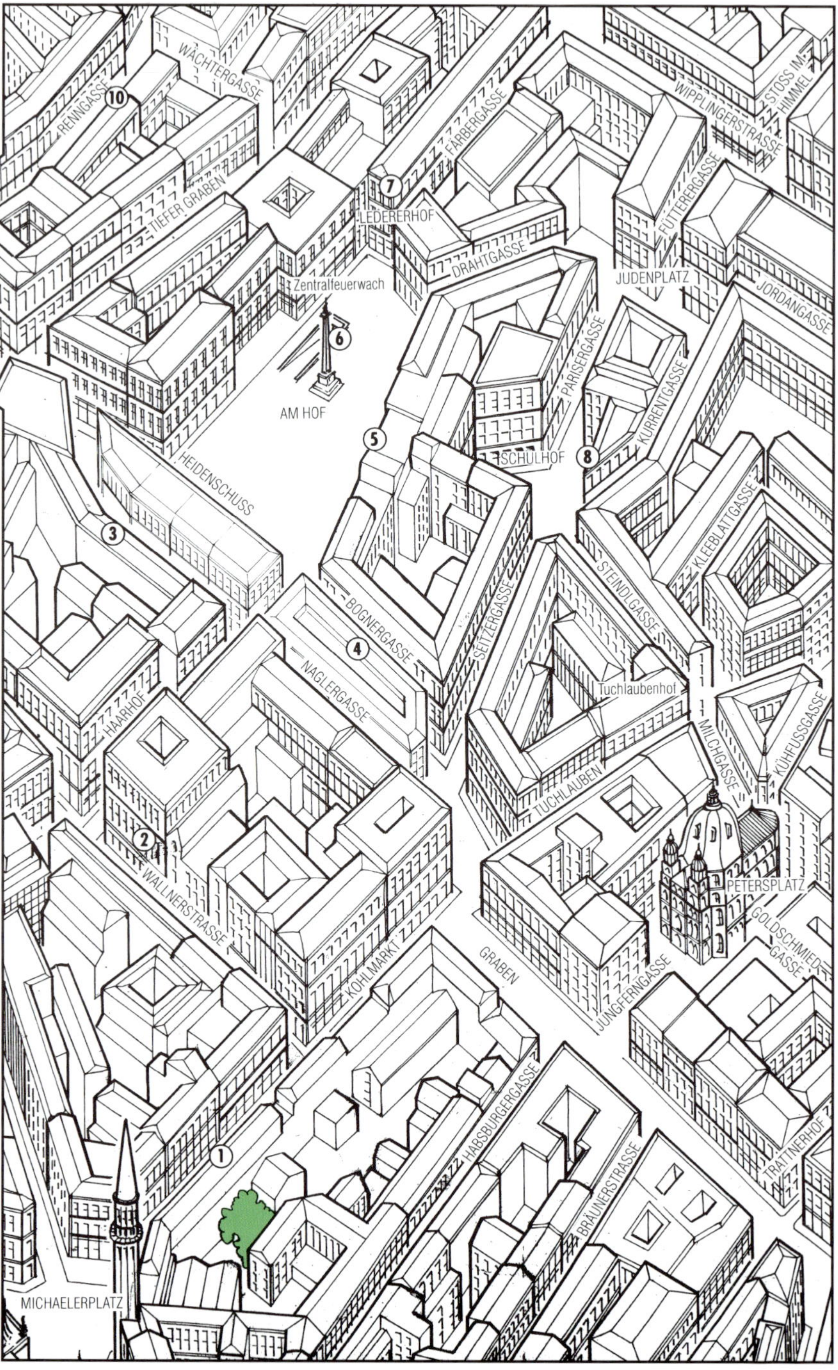

▼ 60/62 ▼ 66

The Kohlmarkt contains fashionable clothes shops, the **Thonet** shop selling its famous bent-wood furniture and ① the best travel and map shop of the city, **Freytag and Berndt** in the *Jugendstil* **Artaria House** at Kohlmarkt 9. The **Esterházy-Palais** ② is at No. 4 Wallnerstrasse. Joseph Haydn's duties as resident composer to the Prince included providing suitable music for the private chapel in the *palais*. ③ A traditional restaurant with Viennese cooking is the **Stadtbeisl** at No. 21 in neighbouring Naglergasse (open 11 am-midnight, **SS**). Something more refined is provided by ④ the fashionable **Schwarzes Kameel** in the parallel Bognergasse at No. 5 (lunch only, **SS**). To one side of Am Hof is ⑤ the **Church of the Nine Choirs of Angels**, its windowed Baroque façade and balcony making it look more like an aristocrat's palace than a church. From the balcony the dissolution of the Holy Roman Empire was announced in 1806. In the middle of the square is ⑥ a **Marian Column** dating from 1667. In the northwestern corner of the square at Am Hof 10 is ⑦ the former **Citizens' Armoury** (now the Central Fire Station) with a splendidly decorated façade. Above it are Lorenzo Mattielli's two allegorical figures (*Steadfastness* and *Strength*) bearing aloft a globe. **The Fire Brigade Museum** is at Am Hof 7. A narrow street leading off Am Hof contains ⑧ the diminutive and charming **Obizzi Palais** (Schulhof 3), which houses the **Clock Museum**, one of the most fascinating of the city's lesser-known sights (open Tue-Sun 9 am-4.30 pm). ⑨ The **Kunstforum**, Renngasse 2, is an exhibition hall in the Bank Austria where seductive shows of 19th and 20thC art are regularly held. At Renngasse 4 is ⑩ the **Schönborn-Batthyány Palais** with a façade by Joseph Emanuel Fischer von Erlach. The Mexican Embassy is one of the occupants.

▲ 38

▲ 36

▲ 48

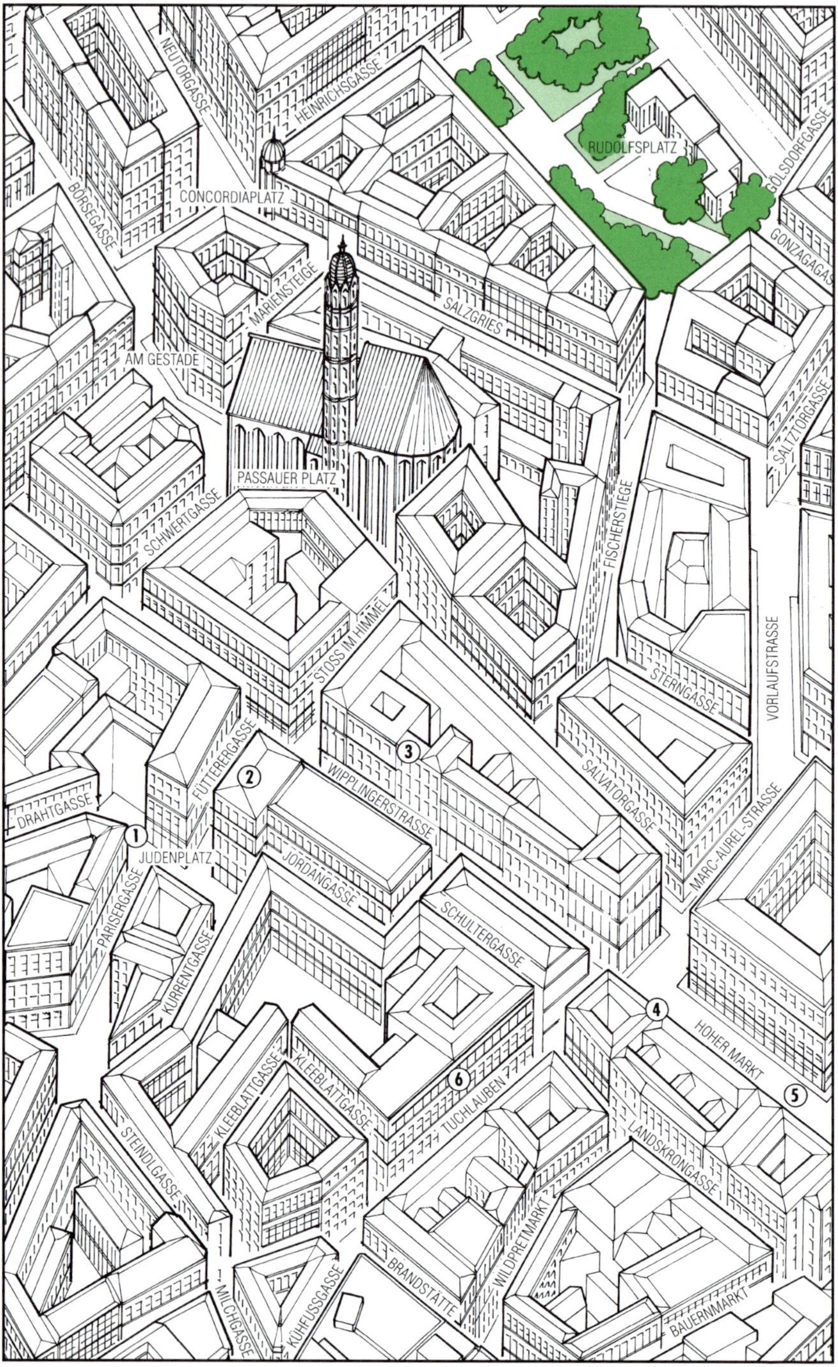
NEUTORGASSE
HEINRICHSGASSE
RUDOLFSPLATZ
GÖLSDORFGASSE
BÖRSEGASSE
CONCORDIAPLATZ
GONZAGAGAS
MARIENSTEIGE
SALZGRIES
AM GESTADE
SALTZTORGASSE
PASSAUER PLATZ
SCHWERTGASSE
FISCHERSTIEGE
STOSS IM HIMMEL
STERNGASSE
VORLAUFSTRASSE
FÜTTERERGASSE
WIPPLINGERSTRASSE
SALVATORGASSE
DRAHTGASSE
MARC-AUREL-STRASSE
JUDENPLATZ
JORDANGASSE
PARISERGASSE
SCHULTERGASSE
KURRENTGASSE
HOHER MARKT
KLEEBLATTGASSE
KLEEBLATTGASSE
TUCHLAUBEN
STEINDLGASSE
LANDSKRONGASSE
WILDPRETMARKT
BRANDSTÄTTE
MILCHGASSE
KÜHFUSSGASSE
BAUERNMARKT
1
2
3
4
5
6

▼ 52

① The **Judenplatz** is where the medieval Jewish ghetto was situated until it was destroyed in a pogrom under Albrecht V in 1421. A relief showing the baptism of Christ on the house of a rich burgher (Great Jordan's House at No. 2) is usually taken to 'commemorate' this awful event, when many Jews were burned alive and others put on a raft and set loose on the Danube. In fact the inscription is a *celebration* of those atrocities which, as it says (in Latin) 'purged the horrible crimes of the Hebrew dogs'. Their main crime was lending money to the nobility, who were then unable or unwilling to pay their debts. One side of ② the **Böhmische Hofkanzlei** (Bohemian Chancellery) looks on to the Judenplatz, the other on to Wipplingerstrasse. The eastern half of the building is Fischer von Erlach's original design. The Constitutional Court is now located here. At No. 8 Wipplingerstrasse is ③ the **Alte Rathaus**, which was the City Hall until 1885. Its façade also recalls Fischer von Erlach (it is probably by his school) and it has a fine Baroque interior. Georg Raphael Donner's **Andromeda Fountain** graces the courtyard. The **District Museum** for the Inner City and the **Museum of the Austrian Resistance Movement** are housed in the building (open Mon, Wed and Thur, 9 am-5 pm). On the nearby **Hoher Markt** are ④ ruins of **Roman officers' houses** at Nos 10-11. In the centre of the Hoher Markt is ⑤ the **Vermählungsbrunnen** (Betrothal Fountain) by Fischer von Erlach the Younger. The sculptural group standing on it is by Antonio Corradini and represents the betrothal of Joseph and Mary. Take the south-west exit into Tuchlauben (in medieval times the cloth market), and you come to ⑥ a small **museum** at No. 19 containing early murals (*circa* 1400) illustrating the bucolic cycle of poems by the Minnesänger Neidhart von Riuwental (open Tue-Sun, 10 am-12.15 pm, 1 pm-4.30 pm).

▲ 50

▲ 48

STOSS IM HIMMEL
JORDANGASSE
STERNGASSE
VORLAUFSTRASSE
FÜTTERERGASSE
WIPPLINGERSTRASSE
SALVATORGASSE
MARC-AUREL-STRASSE
JUDENPLATZ
JORDANGASSE
PARISERGASSE
KURRENTGASSE
SCHULTERGASSE
HOHER MARKT
KLEEBLATTGASSE
TUCHLAUBEN
STEINDLGASSE
LANDSKRONGASSE
WILDPRETMARKT
TUCHLAUBENHOF
1
TUCHLAUBEN
MILCHGASSE
KÜHFUSSGASSE
BAUERNMARKT
2
PETERSPLATZ
BRANDSTÄTTE
KRAMERGASSE
FREISINGERGASSE
JASOMIRGOTTSTRASSE
JUNGFERNGASSE
Hst. Stephansplatz
5
GRABEN
3
TRATTNERHOF
GOLDSCHMIEDGASSE
STEPHANSPLATZ
BRAUNERSTRASSE
DOROTHEERGASSE
4
Hst. Stephansplatz
STOCK-IM-EISEN-PLATZ
Hst. Stephansplatz

▼ 64

① At No. 5 is the **Hochholzerhof**, now owned by a bank that leases out an attractive café in the front part of the beautifully restored Baroque building. Tuchlauben runs to the edge of Graben, off the north side of which is ② Lukas von Hildebrandt's elegant **Peterskirche**, completed in 1716 on the site of two previous churches. Hildebrandt's compact design has triumphed over the drawbacks of the narrow site. The oval interior is packed with fine works: Lorenzo Mattielli's dramatic sculpture of St John Nepomuk being thrown into the Moldau stands out above all else. ③ The **Graben** is the fashionable heart of the Inner City. Originally it was the defensive ditch for the Roman camp, later a market, and later still the beat for high-class prostitutes known in the 18th and 19thC as *Grabennymphen*. The Graben is flanked by neo-Classical, Historicist and *Jugendstil* houses. Interesting modern shop-fronts include that for the jewellers **Schullin** at No. 26 (by Hans Hollein) and for the bookshop **Frick** at No. 27 (Schluder and Kastner, 1988). A superior Konditorei at No. 12, **Lehmann** (open 8.30 am-7 pm, **S**), is well worth a visit. In the middle of the Graben is the magnificent **Plague**, or Holy Trinity Column, designed by Ludovico Burnacini, Fischer von Erlach the Elder and others. Note Paul Strudel's graphic relief on the plinth of Emperor Leopold I kneeling in prayer. At the eastern end of the Graben is ④ Hans Hollein's controversial **Haas Haus** (1990), its rounded steel-and-glass façade picturesquely reflecting St Stephen's opposite. ⑤ **St Stephen's Cathedral** is the finest Gothic building in Austria and its southern tower (the '**Steffl**') is the city's most beloved landmark. The earliest parts of the building (the two **Heidentürme** – 'Heathen Towers' – at the west end) are Romanesque; the rest is mostly Gothic with some Renaissance and Baroque additions. Its graceful **Albertine Choir** was built between 1304 and 1310 and the **South Tower**, perhaps the loveliest in Europe, was begun in 1359. Two great architects, Hans Puchsbaum and Anton Pilgram, stand out from the many who worked on the cathedral. Pilgram's celebrated **pulpit** (1520), at the back of the nave, contains his self-portrait, which is repeated at the foot of the magnificent **organ loft** he designed (1513). At the end of the north aisle is the **Wiener Neustadt Altar** (1447) with panels depicting the life of Mary; and in the south aisle is Niclas Gerhaert van Leyden's stupendous Renaissance **tomb of Friedrich III** (1467). At Stephansplatz 6 is the **Dom-und-Diözesanmuseum**, of which the greatest treasure is the earliest portrait made in the German-speaking world (of Rudolf IV, the Founder).

▲ 38

▲ 50

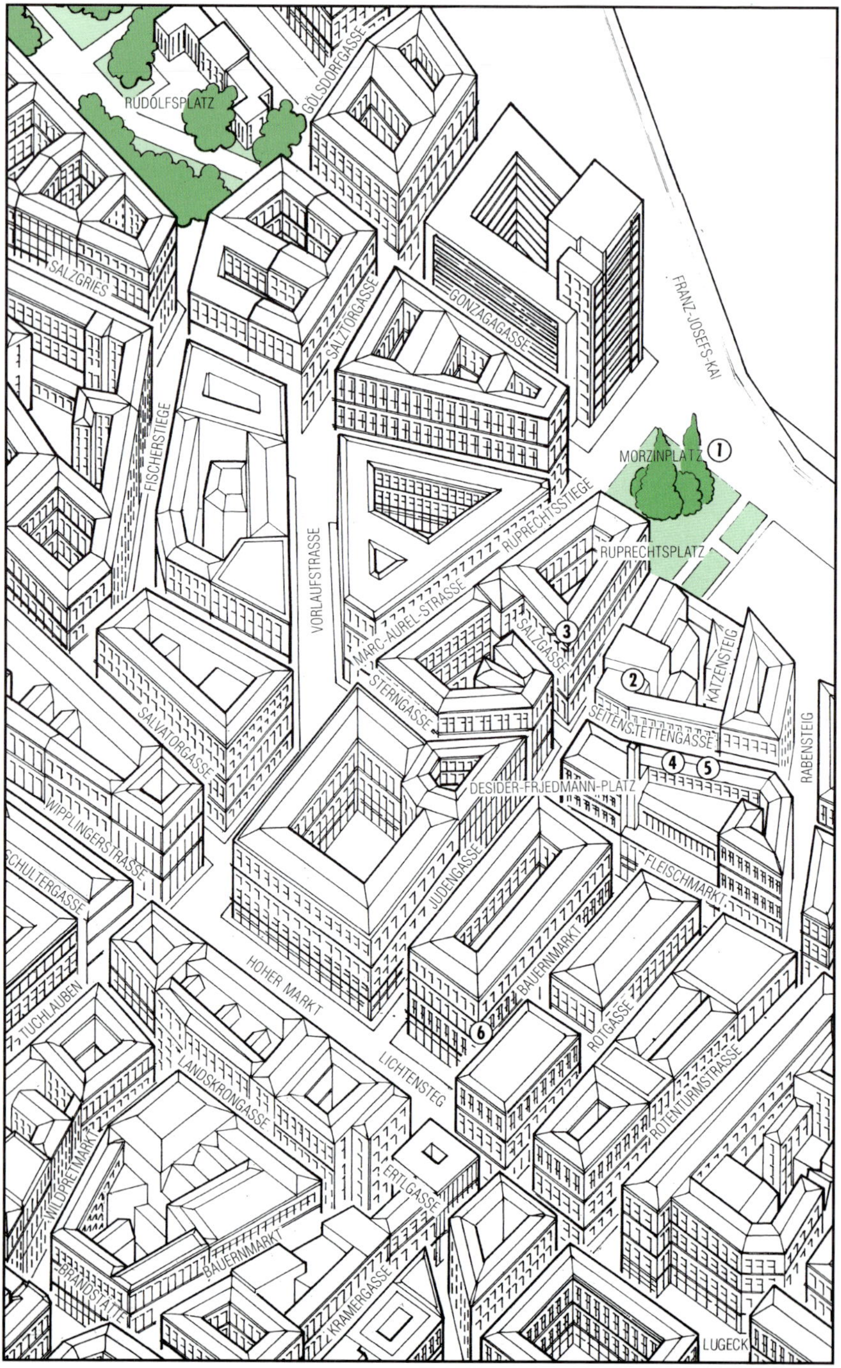
RUDOLFSPLATZ
GÖLSDORFGASSE
SALZGRIES
SALZTORGASSE
GONZAGAGASSE
FRANZ-JOSEFS-KAI
FISCHERSTIEGE
MORZINPLATZ
1
RUPRECHTSSTIEGE
RUPRECHTSPLATZ
VORLAUFSTRASSE
MARC-AUREL-STRASSE
SALZGASSE
3
2
KATZENSTEIG
STERNGASSE
SEITENSTETTENGASSE
RABENSTEIG
SALVATORGASSE
4
5
DESIDER-FRIEDMANN-PLATZ
WIPPLINGERSTRASSE
JUDENGASSE
FLEISCHMARKT
SCHULTERGASSE
BAUERNMARKT
HOHER MARKT
TUCHLAUBEN
6
ROTGASSE
LICHTENSTEG
LANDSKRONGASSE
ROTENTURMSTRASSE
ERTLGASSE
WILDPRETMARKT
BAUERNMARKT
BRANDSTÄTTE
KRAMERGASSE
LUGECK

▼ 52

▼ 56

Morzinplatz (off Franz-Josefs-Kai, alongside the Danube Canal) was formerly the location of the Metropol Hotel, the Gestapo headquarters during the Second World War. The hotel was destroyed by Allied bombing in 1945 and on its site is ① Leopold Grausam's **Monument to the Victims of Fascism** (1985) (off map). The inscription recalls that many Austrian patriots were tortured and murdered here, but also that the building was 'reduced to ruins like the 1,000-year *Reich*'. Climb the steps to ② the ivy-clad **Ruprechtskirche**, whose Romanesque tower reminds us that it is the oldest surviving church in Vienna. St Rupert was the patron saint of the salt miners of the Salzkammergut; since the salt was unloaded on the quay below, it is probable that those in the trade financed the building of the church. The area around Ruprechtsplatz has been patrolled by sten-gun toting police since a terrorist attack on the nearby synagogue in 1982. Nevertheless, these streets are part of the so-called 'Bermuda Triangle', where Vienna's liveliest night-spots are to be found. ③ An 'in' restaurant opposite the church is the **Salzamt** (Ruprechtsplatz 1; open 5 pm-2 am) which boasts excellent cuisine and a fashionable bar. At Seitenstettengasse 2 is ④ the **house** that Joseph Kornhäusel built for himself in 1827, the outstanding feature of which is a rather grim tower that contained his atelier. The tower was extremely difficult of access and the malicious claimed its real purpose was to provide Kornhäusel with a refuge from his overbearing wife. Next door, at Seitenstettengasse 4, is ⑤ the neo-Classical **synagogue** (1826), also designed by Kornhäusel. The exterior, in accordance with Joseph II's regulations concerning non-Catholic places of worship, betrays no sign of the building's function. The oval interior is extremely elegant, with Ionic columns and a ceiling imitating a star-studded sky. Although the synagogue suffered some damage in the *Kristallnacht* (9 November 1938), when Jewish property was looted and burned, it miraculously survived the war more or less unscathed. A turn down Judengasse brings you again to the Hoher Markt. On the archway between the two halves of the Anker Insurance Company's offices is ⑥ Franz Matsch's *Jugendstil* clock (1917), known as the **Ankeruhr**. At midday important figures in Austria's history parade across the clock face, each to the accompaniment of its own signature tune.

▲ 52

▲ 50/52/54

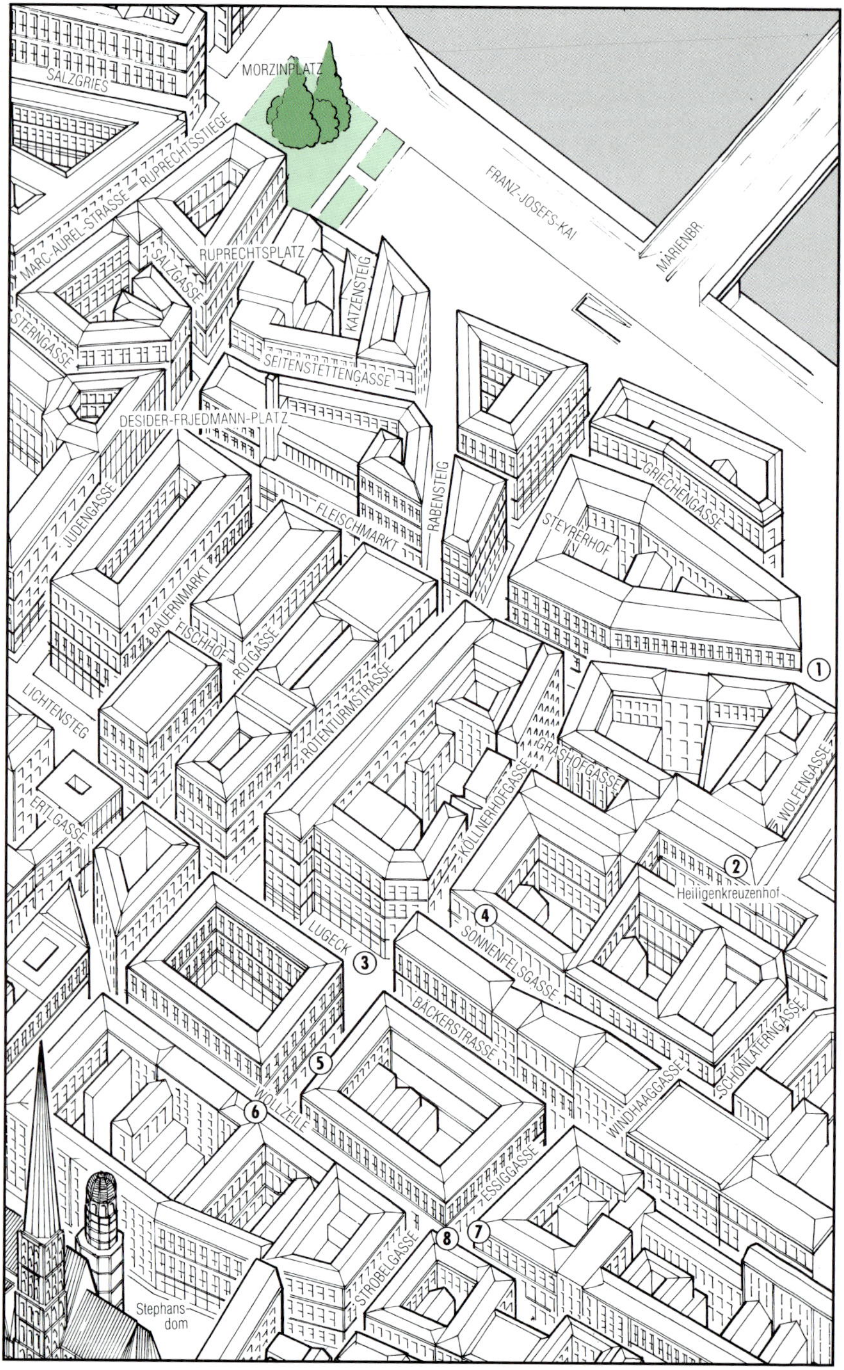

MORZINPLATZ
SALZGRIES
RUPRECHTSSTIEGE
MARC-AUREL-STRASSE
FRANZ-JOSEFS-KAI
MARIENBR.
RUPRECHTSPLATZ
SALZGASSE
KATZENSTEIG
STERNGASSE
SEITENSTETTENGASSE
DESIDER-FRIEDMANN-PLATZ
RABENSTEIG
GRIECHENGASSE
STEYRERHOF
JUDENGASSE
FLEISCHMARKT
BAUERNMARKT
FISCHHOF
ROTGASSE
LICHTENSTEG
ROTENTURMSTRASSE
GRASHOFGASSE
WOLFENGASSE
KÖLLNERHOFGASSE
ERTLGASSE
Heiligenkreuzerhof
SONNENFELSGASSE
LUGECK
BÄCKERSTRASSE
SCHÖNLATERNGASSE
WINDHAAGGASSE
WOLLZEILE
ESSIGGASSE
STROBELGASSE
Stephans-
dom
1
2
3
4
5
6
7
8

▼ 68

The Fleischmarkt, which runs athwart the busy Rotanturmstrasse, is one of the most charming streets of old Vienna. ① No. 11 is the ancient **Griechenbeisl** (off map), one of several restaurants competing for the title of oldest in the city (open 11.30 am-1am, **SSS**). Its most famous regular was the bagpipe-player Augustin, who kept up the spirits of the customers during the terrible plague epidemic of 1679. Leaving the place rather the worse for wear one night, he fell asleep in the street outside and was scooped up by the corpse collectors to be deposited in a mass grave. Fortunately, the burial team went off for its *Pause* (beer-break) before completing the job by pouring in the quicklime. In the meantime Augustin woke up and was able to attract attention by vigorously playing his bagpipes. A little to the south (approached by Köllnerhofgasse and Grashofgasse) is ② the complex of buildings known as the **Heiligenkreuzerhof**. The Cistercians of Heiligenkreuz Abbey outside Vienna acquired land here in the 13thC. An energetic Abbot, Clemens Schäffer, commissioned the present Baroque buildings in 1659 and further alterations were made in the 18thC. Nearby is Lugeck, in the centre of which is ③ a **monument** to the inventor of movable type, Johann Gutenberg. At Sonnenfelsgasse 3 is a house designed by Lukas von Hildebrandt (1721), below which are three levels of ④, the **Zwölf Apostel-keller** (Twelve Apostles wine cellar, **S**). The deepest level is medieval. It is open 4.30 pm to midnight and popular with students as the wine is a reasonable price. Off Lugeck is Bäckerstrasse, and an alley runs from it into Wollzeile. On the other side ⑤ is the celebrated **Figlmüller**, whose waiters are renowned for their wit, and which serves the biggest and best *Wienerschnitzel* in town (open daily 11 am-10 pm, **SS**). Figlmüller also owns the little wine bar opposite, **Vis-à-Vis** – thirty-five wines on offer, all available by the glass (**S**). Opposite as you exit on to Wollzeile is ⑥ the city's most elegant delicatessen, **Schönbichler**, selling, amongst other things, English teas and marmalades. Turn left down the street and pop into ⑦ No. 11, the book emporium of **Morawa**. Apart from a vast stock of German books it sells a number of newspapers and magazines in English, for which it is the importer and distributor. ⑧ **Café Diglas** opposite it is a recently-restored, atmospheric traditional café with decent food (Wollzeile 10; open 7 am-11.30 pm).

▲ 44

▲ 92

Volks Garten
3
5
HELDENPLATZ
6
Burgtor
4
2
BURGRING
Neue Hofburg
1
Kunsthistorisches Museum

▼ 100

The Museum of Art History/Heldenplatz

① The **Kunsthistorischen Museum** (Museum of Art History) faces the Natural History Museum across Maria-Theresien-Platz. Gottfried Semper had incorporated the museum into his mega-plan for a *'Kaiserforum'* (*see page 93*), but the original winner of a competition for the design of the building itself was Karl von Hasenauer. He was obliged to work with Semper, but the two fell out and Hasenauer completed the task alone. The official opening was in 1891. Until then the vast Habsburg art collection had been scattered throughout the imperial buildings. The collection includes Egyptian and Oriental antiquities, coins and medals, goldsmiths' and silversmiths' work, astrological instruments, clocks and, above all, pictures. The museum is open Tue, Wed, Fri-Sun, 10 am-6 pm, Sat 9 am-4 pm. Extended hours to 9 pm on Thursday. Across the Ringstrasse is the rest of Gottfried Semper's half-realized *'Kaiserforum'*. To the right is ② the somewhat bombastic **Neue Hofburg**, which should have been complemented (according to Semper's plan) by a similar building facing it. Various architects (including Hasenauer) worked on the project, which was eventually completed by Ludwig Baumann in 1913. It houses the main part of the **National Library** and the **Museum für Völkerkunde** (Ethnology Museum). The museum is open Mon, Wed-Sun, 10 am-4 pm. From the Balcony of the Neue Hofburg Hitler addressed cheering crowds on the Heldenplatz shortly after his annexation of Austria (the *Anschluss*) in 1938. The square is flanked on the north side by ③ the elegant Baroque wing of the Hofburg known as the **Leopoldinische Trakt** after the Emperor Leopold I in whose reign it was built. The first building (1666) by Filiberto Lucchesi was burned down and rebuilt (1681) by Domenico Carlone. At the western end is the entrance to the Presidential Apartments, currently occupied by the newly-elected Thomas Klestil, who replaced the discredited Kurt Waldheim. The state rooms (not open to the public) have impressive Baroque decoration. Dominating the Heldenplatz are two monumental equestrian statues. On the Neue Hofburg side is ④ that to **Prince Eugene of Savoy** (1663-1736), the hero of the Turkish wars. On the Volksgarten side is ⑤ the much more successful and dramatic monument to **Archduke Carl** (1771-1847), the victor against Napoleon at the Battle of Aspern (1809). On the Ringstrasse side of the Heldenplatz is ⑥ the great **Burgtor** (1824), built on the orders of Franz I in memory of the Battle of the Nations at Leipzig (1813) that marked the beginning of the end for Napoleon.

▲ 46 ▲ 48

MICHAELERPLATZ
HABSBURGERGASSE
REITSCHULGASSE
BRÄUNERSTRASSE
STALLBURGGASSE
Alte Hofburg
BRÄUNERSTRASSE
JOSEFSPLATZ
Nationalbibliothek
DOROTHEERGASSE
Neue Hofburg
AUGUSTINERSTRASSE
AUGUSTINERBASTEI
LOBKOWITZPLATZ
Albertina
Burggarten
GOETHEGASSE
HANUSCHGASSE
ALBERTINAPLATZ

▲ 58

▼ 102

① The delightful, intimate **Burggarten** behind the Neue Hofburg was laid out by Louis von Remy in 1818. The earliest glasshouse was built here in 1826, but was replaced by Friedrich Ohmann's present construction in 1907, which combines *Jugendstil* with Historicism. Also in the garden is a Baroque equestrian statue of Franz Stephan of Lorraine (Maria Theresa's husband) by Balthasar Moll (1780) and a bronze of Franz Joseph. The romanticized representation of Mozart by Viktor Tilgner (1896) is a magnet for visitors. Beyond the garden and the Neue Hofburg are ② the other wings of the enormous **Hofburg**. An archway from the Heldenplatz leads into a courtyard bounded (on one side) by the **Leopoldinische Trakt** (*see page 59*), the **Amalienhof** at the north-western end, and to the north-east the **Reichskanzleitrakt**, where the offices for the administration of the Empire were situated. You can also see the Renaissance **Schweizertor** (the Swiss Gate, so called because Swiss Guards were employed in the 18thC), which leads to the oldest parts of the Burg. Access to the **Burgkapelle** (1499, but baroque-ized later) is from the southern corner: the Vienna Boys' Choir performs a sung mass here at 9.15 am on Sun, Jan-Jun and mid-Sep to mid-Dec. Below is the entrance to the **Schatzkammer** (Treasury, open Wed-Mon, 10 am-6 pm), containing the crown and insignia of the Holy Roman Empire. Retrace your steps through the Schweizertor and enter the Imperial Apartments from the main courtyard (left of cupola). The apartments are open daily 9 am-5 pm. Going through the archway, you reach the Michaelerplatz and ③ the Gothic **Michaelerkirche** dating from the late 14thC, with Baroque additions. The lively sculptural group over the portal (St Michael casting out a rebel angel) is by Lorenzo Mattielli (1724). The relief of fallen angels over the high altar is impressively theatrical. To one side of the church an archway leads into the Josefsplatz. You pass the lovely Renaissance **Stallburg** (1558), home to the celebrated Lipizzaners; opposite is the **Spanish Riding School** and the **Redoute** (once used for balls during the Congress of Vienna in 1814, of which it was said *"le Congrès ne marche pas, il danse"*.) The Redoute is still under repair after the fire of 1992, but the Lipizzaners are back at work. In the middle of the Josefsplatz is ④ an **equestrian statue** (1807) by Franz Anton Zauner of the rationalist Emperor Joseph II. ⑤ is the **Hofbibliothek** (1735), designed and built by the Fischer von Erlachs, father and son.

▲ 46 ▲ 48

▲ 58

▲ 64

▼ 102

On the north-east side of the square are two Baroque palaces, ① of the **Pallavicinis** at No. 5 and ② of the **Pálffys** at No. 6. The original owner of No. 5 was forced to add a pretentious portal and roof sculpture to his palace because its features were considered too mean for the vicinity of the Hofburg. Fans of Carol Reed's famous movie *The Third Man* will recognize its façade, in front of which Harry Lime's naïve friend was nearly mown down (on purpose?) by a car. Continue south and you will reach ③ the Gothic **Augustinerkirche** (Church of the Augustinian Friars). Its most spectacular work of art is Antonio Canova's cenotaph (1805) for Maria Theresa's favourite daughter, Marie Christine. In the church's vault the hearts of the Habsburg rulers are preserved in silver urns. Sunday's sung mass here is often a performance of a work by Haydn or Mozart with full orchestra. Beyond the church is ④ the **Albertina**, housing the world's greatest collection of drawings and graphics (open 10 am-4 pm, with shorter hours on Friday and at weekends). At the far end of the building is the **Danube Fountain** (1869) featuring allegories of the rivers of Austria; above it is the **monument** to Archduke Albrecht, victor against the Italians at Custozza in 1866. In the middle of Albertinaplatz is ⑤ Alfred Hrdlicka's controversial **Monument against War and Fascism**, erected in 1988 in the fiftieth anniversary year of the *Anschluss*. Around the corner to the west of the Albertina in Hanuschgasse (at No. 3) is ⑥ one part of the **Theatre Museum**. ⑦ The rest of the Theatre Museum has recently been installed in the **Lobkowitz-Palais** (Lobkowitzplatz 2) to the north of the Augustinerkirche (open Tue-Sat, 9 am-12.30 pm, 1.30 pm-5 pm; Sun, 9 am-1 pm). The palace was built by Giovanni Tencala in 1687 and the façade altered by Fischer von Erlach the Elder in 1710. In its subsequently-named 'Eroicasaal', Beethoven conducted the first performance of this symphony for his patron, Prince Lobkowitz, in 1804. Just to the west is the Dorotheergasse. ⑧ At Nos 18 and 16 are **two churches** of different Protestant communities, built on the site of a Clarissan convent after Joseph II allowed freedom of religion with his Edict of Tolerance (1781). At No. 17 Dorotheergasse is ⑨ the state auction house's main hall, known as the **Dorotheum**. It was founded by Joseph I and under Joseph II moved into its present building, formerly the convent of the Dorothean nuns. Refreshment for the weary is at hand in ⑩ the nearby **Bräunerhof Café**, where concerts and literary events sometimes take place.

▲ 52

▲ 48

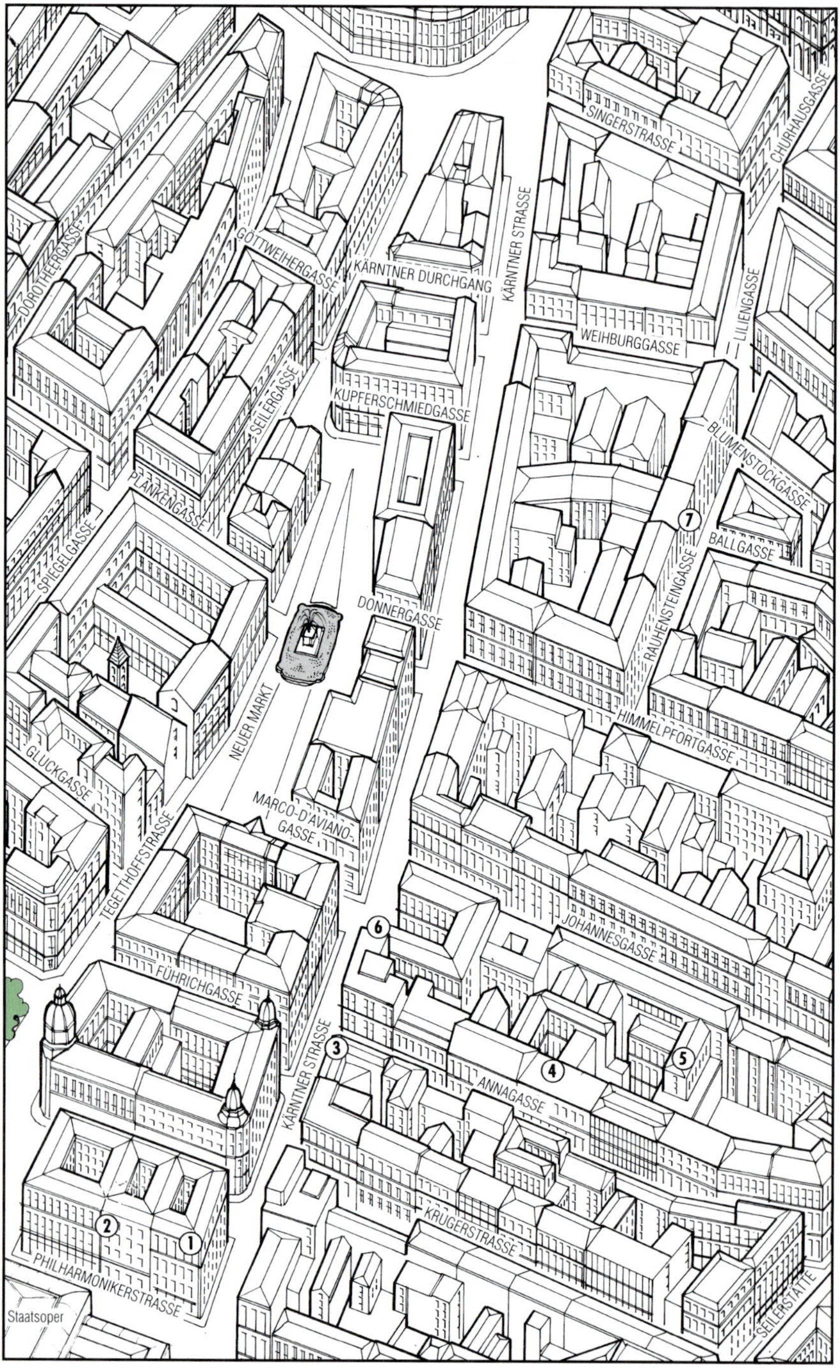

SINGERSTRASSE
CHURHAUSGASSE
KÄRNTNER STRASSE
DOROTHEERGASSE
GÖTTWEIHERGASSE
KÄRNTNER DURCHGANG
LILIENGASSE
WEIHBURGGASSE
SEILERGASSE
KUPFERSCHMIEDGASSE
BLUMENSTOCKGASSE
PLANKENGASSE
SPIEGELGASSE
7
BALLGASSE
RAUHENSTEINGASSE
DONNERGASSE
NEUER MARKT
HIMMELPFORTGASSE
GLUCKGASSE
MARCO-D'AVIANO-GASSE
TEGETTHOFFSTRASSE
JOHANNESGASSE
6
FÜHRICHGASSE
3
KÄRNTNER STRASSE
4
5
ANNAGASSE
KRUGERSTRASSE
2
1
PHILHARMONIKERSTRASSE
Staatsoper
SEILERSTÄTTE

▼ 104

The historic Kärntner Strasse, once the main road to Carinthia and the south, is now a pedestrian zone between the opera house and St Stephan's Cathedral. It is Vienna's best-known shopping mall. At the opera end, on the left (No. 38) as you enter the street, is ① the **Fremdenverkehrsstelle der Stadt Wien** (Tourist Information Office), which has brochures, programmes and other information. Behind it, at Philharmonikerstrasse 4 is the famous **Hotel Sacher** ②, from which the cake takes its name. Across the street at No. 41 is ③ the diminutive **Esterházy-Palais**, (one of two in Vienna) built in the mid-17thC and altered in 1785. On the upper floor a casino now operates. Turn into Annagasse and you come upon ④ **Annakirche** (St Anne's Church, 1747) at No. 3B. A fine ceiling fresco by Daniel Gran represents the Immaculate Conception, and Gran was also the artist for the altarpiece (The Holy Family). In a side chapel is a late-Gothic wooden sculpture (1510) by Master Veit of Nürnberg (The Virgin Mary, the Child Jesus and St Anne). ⑤ Located at Annagasse 5/Johannesgasse 6 is the **Hofkammerarchiv** (Imperial Archive) that still houses many records of the Empire in neatly-tied fascicles. On the second floor is the office of the playwright Franz Grillparzer, preserved as he had it when he was director of the archive . It is usually possible to visit the rooms if you apply at the Johannesgasse entrance. Return to Kärntner Strasse and make your way to ⑥, No. 37, the **Malteser Kirche** of the Knights of St John, who came to Vienna in the 13thC under Leopold VI, the Glorious, of Babenberg. The small church dates to that time but was altered in neo-Classical style in 1808, probably by Louis von Montoyer. The current Grand Master of the order is an Englishman. Across the street at No. 30 is Vienna's best specialist bookshop for works on art and architecture, **Georg Prachner**, and next to it the **Columbia Music Shop** on three floors. Nearby, on the other side of the street at No. 33, is **Joh Backhausen & Söhne**, original producers of textiles for the Wiener Werkstätte, whose pattern books they retain. At No. 26 (opposite) is the famous glass firm of **Lobmeyer**, founded in 1823. In the narrow Rauhensteingasse ⑦ at No. 8 is the site of the **house where Mozart died** on December 5th 1791. There is a memorial room.

▲ 52

▲ 64

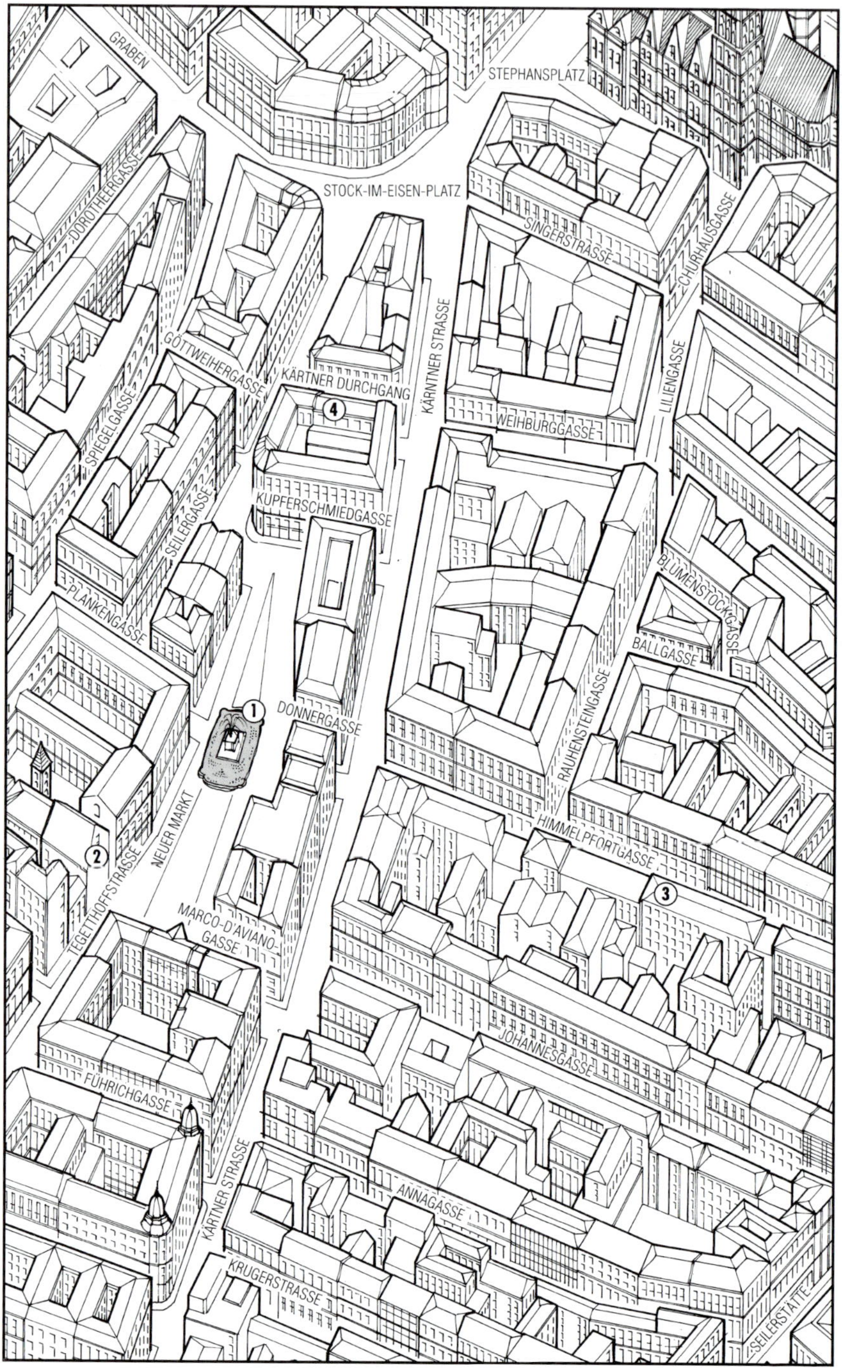
GRABEN
STEPHANSPLATZ
STOCK-IM-EISEN-PLATZ
DOROTHEERGASSE
SINGERSTRASSE
CHURHAUSGASSE
KÄRNTNER STRASSE
LILIENGASSE
GÖTTWEIHERGASSE
KÄRTNER DURCHGANG
SPIEGELGASSE
4
WEIHBURGGASSE
SEILERGASSE
KUPFERSCHMIEDGASSE
BLUMENSTOCKGASSE
PLANKENGASSE
BALLGASSE
1
DONNERGASSE
RAUHENSTEINGASSE
NEUER MARKT
HIMMELPFORTGASSE
2
TEGETTHOFFSTRASSE
3
MARCO-D'AVIANO-GASSE
JOHANNESGASSE
FÜHRICHGASSE
KÄRNTNER STRASSE
ANNAGASSE
KRUGERSTRASSE
SEILERSTÄTTE

▼ 64

① On the **Neuen Markt** is an 1873 copy of Raphael Donner's **Providentia Fountain**: the original, made 1739, is in the Baroque museum of the Lower Belvedere. Providence sits on a plinth surrounded by personifications of the rivers bordering Lower Austria. The naked putti around the base were removed on the orders of a shocked Maria Theresa in 1773 but replaced in 1801. On the west side of the Neuen Markt are ② the **Kapuzinergruft** and **Kapuzinerkirche** (Imperial Vault and Capuchin church). The Capuchins came to Vienna in 1599 and were asked by Anna of Tyrol, wife of Emperor Matthias, to found a monastery on the Mehlmarkt, as it then was. The founder and her husband were also the first Habsburgs to be laid to rest in the Imperial Vault beneath the church, beginning a tradition that continued (with some exceptions) up to the burial of the ex-Empress Zita in 1989. Although the bodies of the rulers are deposited here, their hearts are kept in the Augustinerkirche (*see page 63*) and their embalmed entrails in the catacombs of St Stephan's Cathedral. The Capuchin vault is one of the highlights of a visit to Vienna, containing superb tombs by some of the greatest Baroque masters. The most famous is Balthasar Moll's double sarcophagus (1753) for Maria Theresa and her husband Franz Stephan. Scenes from their lives are featured in reliefs on the side and they themselves are represented on the lid, gazing steadfastly into each other's eyes. In Himmelpfortgasse you come to ③ Prince Eugene of Savoy's **Winter Palace** (No. 8). The building was planned and begun by Fischer von Erlach the Elder (1698), but continued and altered by Lukas von Hildebrandt (1709). The reliefs of mythological scenes on the façade are by Lorenzo Mattielli; the decorative theme of the interior features Hercules and Apollo. The palace (sometimes open for exhibitions) now belongs to the Finance Ministry. Another street off Kärntner Strasse is the Weihburggasse, containing two famous restaurants (at Nos 4 and 6), **Zu den drei Husaren** (**SSS**) and **Zum weissen Rauchfangkehrer** (**SS**). The former offers luxury cuisine in elegant surroundings, the latter Viennese cooking in a rustic interior. Further down towards the Ring is the **British Bookshop**. On the other side of Kärntner Strasse, in the alleyway known as the Kärntner Durchgang, is ④ the famous **Kärntner Bar** (American bar, **S**, 1909), designed by Adolf Loos. The tiny space is made to seem larger than it is by the mirror walls. Sumptuous features include a mahogany counter, a black-and-white marble floor and slabs of transparent onyx over the windows.

▲ 56

▲ 64/66

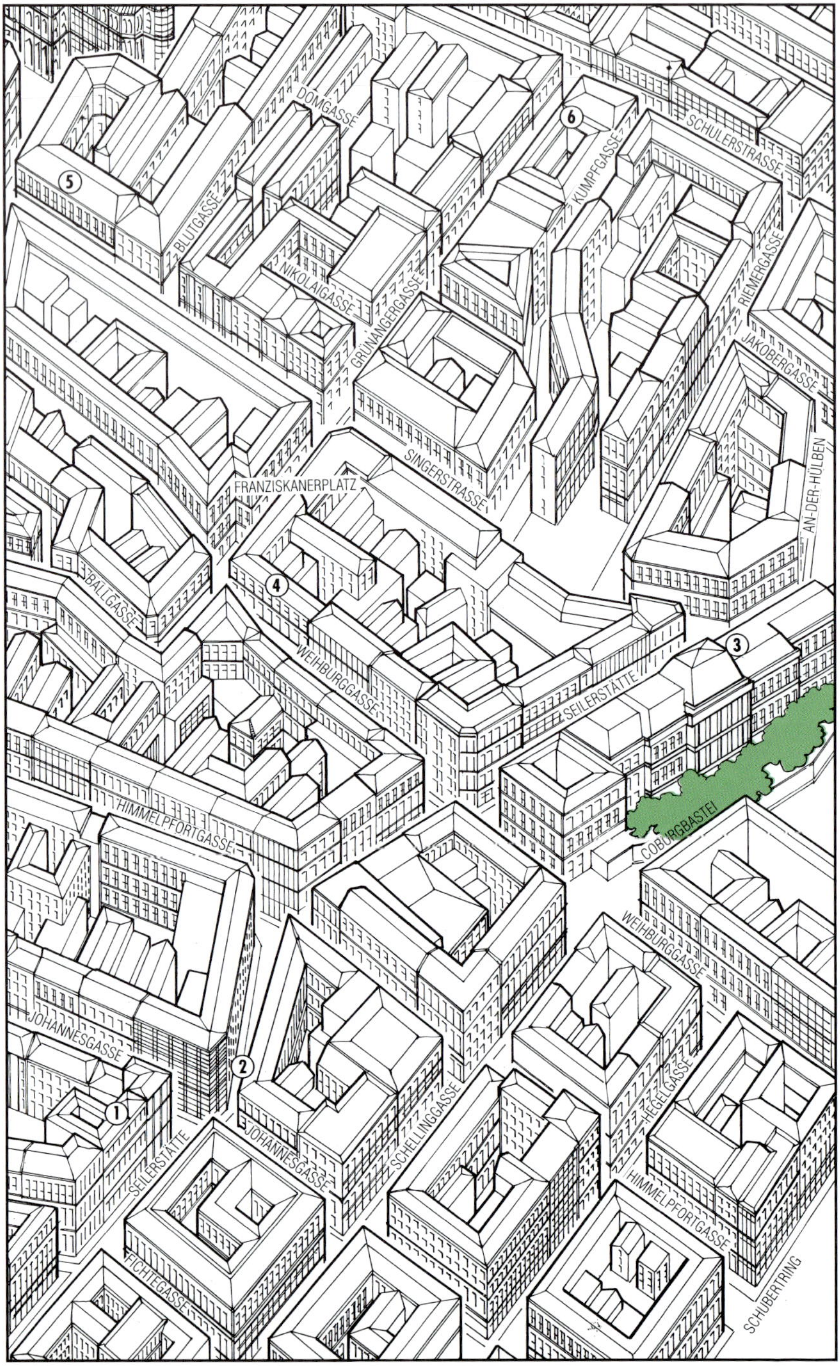
DOMGASSE
SCHULERSTRASSE
KUMPFGASSE
BLUTGASSE
NIKOLAIGASSE
GRÜNANGERGASSE
RIEMERGASSE
JAKOBERGASSE
SINGERSTRASSE
AN-DER-HÜLBEN
FRANZISKANERPLATZ
BALLGASSE
WEIHBURGGASSE
SEILERSTÄTTE
HIMMELPFORTGASSE
COBURGBASTEI
WEIHBURGGASSE
JOHANNESGASSE
HEGELGASSE
SCHELLINGGASSE
JOHANNESGASSE
SEILERSTÄTTE
HIMMELPFORTGASSE
FICHTEGASSE
SCHUBERTRING
1
2
3
4
5
6

▼ 106

Franziskanerplatz and Neighbourhood

① In Johannesgasse, a long Baroque Building divided by a church was formerly the **Ursuline Convent**. The High School for Music has been situated in the eastern wing since 1960. The church acquired a massive new organ in 1968 and is sometimes a concert venue. ② In Seilerstätte, No. 9 is the **Ronacher Etablissement** built by Fellner and Hellmer (1888) as a variety theatre, (now a venue for musicals), with a hotel attached. Beyond it is the Coburg Bastei, behind which is ③ the **Coburg-Palais**, Seilerstätte 1, built in late neo-Classical style in 1842. It has been divided into apartments which enjoy a legally-enshrined right to a view of the Ring and the Stadtpark beyond. West of the Seilerstätte lies the Franziskanerplatz with ④ the **Franciscan church**, a curious mixture of Gothic and South German Renaissance, particularly the façade. The adjacent Franciscan monastery (1622) is built on the site of a house for reformed prostitutes, founded in 1347. It also operated as a kind of marriage bureau – the Viennese bourgeoisie were encouraged to take these women as wives. Parallel to Weihburggasse is Singerstrasse. ⑤ At nearby Singerstrasse no. 7 (Stephansplatz 4) are the **Deutschordenshaus** and **church**, the Viennese seat of the Teutonic Knights since 1200. The picturesque courtyard is bounded to the west by two storeys of glassed-in corridors – what the Viennese call a *Pawlatschen* house. Impressive gravestones of members of the order line the walls of the Gothic church. In the adjoining house you can visit the Knights' Treasury; admission times vary – it is best to check: tel. 512 10 65/6. ⑥ The **Neuberger Hof** Grünangergasse (No. 1) is one of the oldest houses in the city, albeit altered over the centuries. On the second floor the famous **Galerie nächst St Stephan** was founded in 1954 by Monsignor Otto Mauer, a charismatic liberal Catholic in the post-war era. His open-mindedness towards modern art, hitherto viewed with suspicion by the church, caused a tremendous stir. Close by in the Schulerstrasse (but off map) is the **Hotel König von Ungarn** (No. 10, **SS**), a tasteful adaptation of a 16thC building. The central courtyard with a glassed-in roof makes a pleasant bar and sitting area and there is a first-class restaurant (**SSS**). In the 19thC nobles visiting Vienna often used to put up at the hotel, famous for its cuisine. Next door is the **Figarohaus**, now partly a museum (entrance at Domgasse 5). Mozart lived in the house between 1784 and 1787 and composed *The Marriage of Figaro* here.

① The **Chemical Institute** at the end of Boltzmanngasse (off map) partly occupies the site of a 16thC bakery, turned into an invalids' home under Maria Theresa. An otherwise inexplicable Viennese insult ("*Der g'hört ins Bäckenhäusel*" "he should be put in the bakery") is a folk memory of this. Boltzmanngasse itself is named after the distinguished physicist, Ludwig Boltzmann (1844-1906).

Liechtenstein-Gartenpalais 'in der Rossau'

The Strudlhofgasse ends with ② the **Strudlhofstiege**, a beautiful art nouveau flight of steps designed by Theodor Jäger in 1910 that descends to the Liechtensteinstrasse. Its name recalls the court painter, Peter von Strudel, who built a substantial residence nearby (1690) where the Academy of Artists (of which he was the founder and first director) was housed. Later the building was used as a plague hospital, before the plot was broken up for rented apartments. The Strudlhofstiege has achieved fame as the setting for Heimito von Doderer's novel (1951) of the same name, a panorama of middle-class Viennese life in the first half of this century. (The District Museum at Währinger Strasse 43 has a room dedicated to Doderer; *see page 51.*) At the bottom of the steps is ...

The Strudlhofstiege

③ the noble **Liechtenstein Gartenpalais** (Liechtenstein Summer Palace) 'in the Rossau': the appellation *Rossau*, earlier *Rosstrenk*, refers to the fact that here, in the periodically flooded meadows that once covered the area, the Danube shipmen used to water their horses. Prince Hans Adam von Liechtenstein employed Domenico Martinelli, Antonio Riva and Lorenz Laher to build the monumental Baroque palace (1704). The *sala terrena* is decorated with medallions painted by Johann Michael Rottmayr. A splendid stairway leads up to the Ceremonial Hall, on the ceiling of which is Andrea Pozzo's depiction of the *Apotheosis of Hercules*. In the garden Johann Bernhard Fischer von Erlach built a 'belvedere', which was replaced by a new building in 1875. Originally the Liechtensteins kept their private picture collection in the palace, but the pictures were moved to Vaduz during the Second World War. Since 1979 the building has been rented by the state and houses the Museum of Modern Art.

Liechtenstein Gartenpalais

① The **Allegemeine Krankenhaus**, entered from Spitalgasse and Alser Strasse, is a vast complex of medical institutes broken up by a large garden courtyard and 12 smaller ones beyond it. Emperor Leopold I began building a hospital on this site in 1693 for the veterans of the Turkish wars; but it was Joseph II who, in 1784, employed two distinguished architects, Isidor Canevale and Matthias Gerl, to create a large hospital inspired by the Hôtel Dieu in Paris. On the south side of Spitalgasse, a new Pathological Anatomical Institute was opened in 1914, which was to become the focus of the world-famous Viennese Medical School in the inter-war years. The science of medicine has a long and distinguished history in the city, starting with the reforms introduced by Maria Theresa's physician, Gerhard van Swieten, a

▲ 70

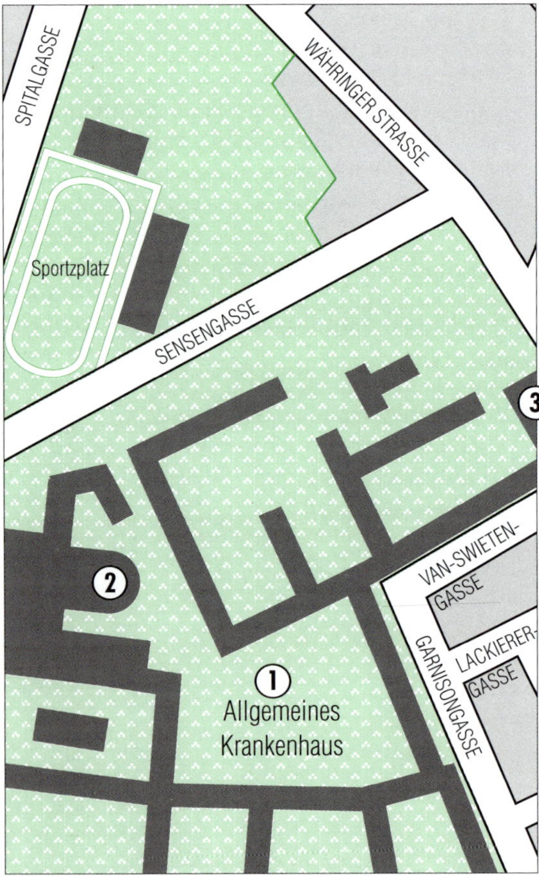

▶ 76

▼ 30

pupil of the great Dutch physician Boerhaave. The 19thC also threw up distinguished figures, such as the surgeon Theodor Billroth and Ignac Semmelweis, who discovered the cause of puerperal fever. Viennese doctors were famous for their brilliance in diagnosis, which became something of an obsession, leading (it is claimed) to an apparent disinterest in effective treatment. Stretching beyond the Institute to the west is the huge scandal-ridden modern hospital. Construction began in 1964 but was repeatedly interrupted by corruption trials involving politicians and contractors. In the sixth courtyard of the old hospital (entrance Spitalgasse 2) is ...

② the celebrated cylindrical **Narrenturm** (Lunatics' Tower), now the **Pathologisch-Anatomisches Bundesmuseum** (Pathological-Anatomical Museum). This was originally an asylum for the insane with five storeys each containing 28 cells. In popular parlance it was known as Kaiser-Josephs-Gugelhupf (Emperor Joseph's Pound Cake – on account of its shape) and the Viennese are still fond of remarking that this or that spectacularly fatuous politician should be "put in the Gugelhupf". The museum on the first floor is concerned with pathogeny and includes gruesome displays of lungs eaten away by smoking, assorted horrors of skin disease and a world-beating collection of gall- and kidney-stones; there is a freshly opened section on venereal diseases and AIDS. Just the thing before lunch. (Open Wed 3-6 pm, Thur 8-11 am, first Sat of the month 10 am-1 pm; closed Aug and holidays.) Make your way to Währinger Strasse and you come to ...

③ the **Josephinum** at No. 25, built in 1785 on the orders of Joseph II to train army surgeons. Isidor Canevale was the architect. The library contains the Museum of the History of Medicine: the star attractions are the marvellous wax figures used for anatomical instruction.

Joseph II

The main traffic artery of Währinger Strasse sweeps through the university medical quarter up to the Gürtel (ring road). At No. 10 on the corner with Türkenstrasse ① the first **Chemical Institute** (off map) was built in restrained neo-Renaissance style by Heinrich Ferstel (1872). It is a far more attractive building than the overblown neo-Baroque of the second Chemical Institute at No. 38, built in 1913. *See also page 70.* The Wasagasse runs parallel to the first part of Währinger Strasse; here too the ubiquitous Ferstel was active, building houses at ...

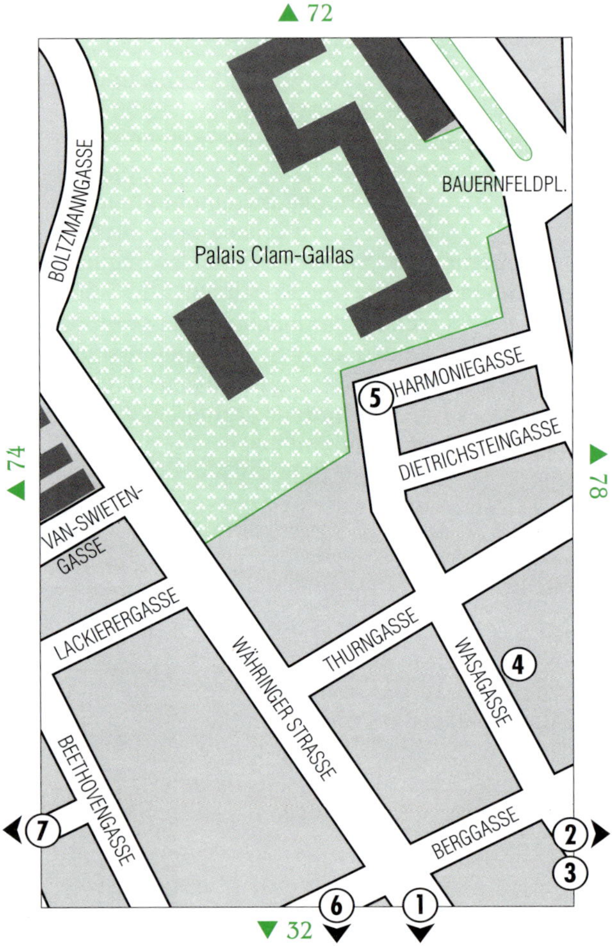

② **No. 2** and at ③ No. 10 (corner of Hörlgasse; both off map). The latter is the **Maximiliansgymnasium**, a school with attractive brickwork features. At No. 22 are ...

④ the comfortable new offices of the **Fremdenpolizei**, less daunting to visit than their previous crumbling headquarters on the Fleischmarkt.

⑤ The '**Harmoniegasse**' is a reminder that the Harmonie Theatre formerly stood at Wasagasse 33. Founded in 1865 and boasting an interior by Otto Wagner (later the leading architect of the Viennese Secession), economic circumstances forced it to become an 'Orpheum' (variety theatre) in 1868. Although it later reverted to straight theatre, it had to close in 1928 and was demolished to make way for houses. To the south of Währinger Strasse, opposite Berggasse, the Schwarzspanierstrasse runs south with the Beethovengasse and Garnisongasse leading off it.

⑥ **Schwarzspanierstrasse 15** (off map) is the site of the house in which Beethoven died in March 1827. Otto Weininger, author of a notoriously sexist and anti-semitic tract entitled *Sex and Character*, made a spectacular exit by committing suicide in the Beethoven House in 1903 (then still the original building). It had been the prelacy office of the Schwarzspanier order (reformed Benedictines, mostly from Spain, who wore black robes).

⑦ Their **church** was at Garnisongasse 14-16 (off map), and had a chequered history. It was burned down as part of the scorched earth strategy used against the besieging Turks in 1683, but afterwards rebuilt. Later it was used as a military stores, then again as a church for the Lutherans, and for the Russian Orthodox community (1930-1938). Since 1966 it has been a Protestant students' college, Albert Schweitzer House. At Währinger Strasse 18 is a new Turkish restaurant, **Lokanta Sarikoç**, which is excellent value for money (**S**, open daily 11 am-midnight).

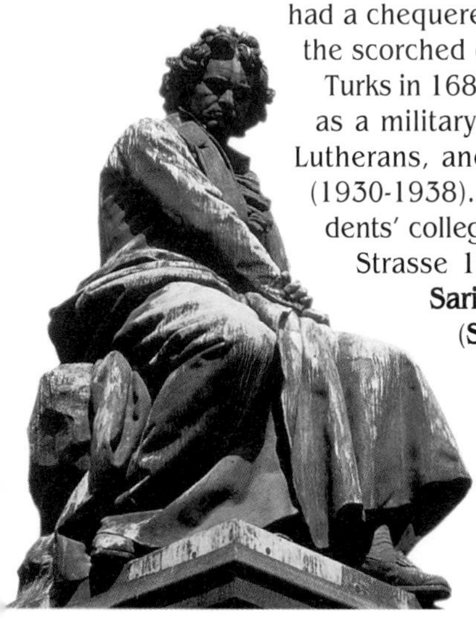

Beethoven

① In the Servitengasse at No. 9 is the **Baroque church** built for the Italian order of Servites in the 1670s. The first architect was Carlo Canevale. The building was altered by Francesco Martinelli in 1684 and in 1727 the Peregrini Chapel was begun. The Servite saint to whom the chapel is dedicated was a truculent individual who once struck the prior of the order, Philip Benizi, in the course of a heated argument. However he was so impressed by the latter's relaxed and peaceful response to this act of aggression that he decided to join the Servites himself. The chapel possesses a shrine with healing powers over foot ailments – one of the supplicants who sought relief here was Joseph Haydn. The interior of the main church is richly decorated with Baroque trappings.

▲ 76

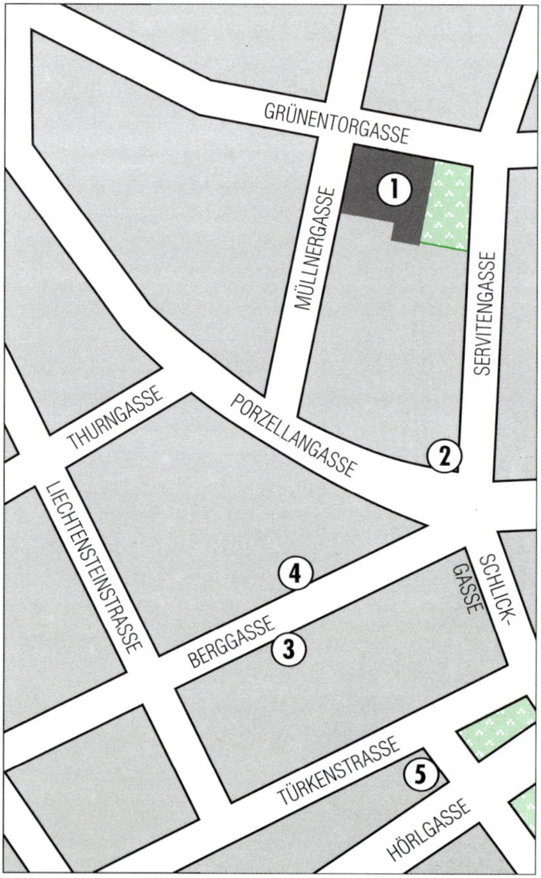

80 ▼

▼ 34

② An imposing house on the corner of Porzellangasse and Servitengasse is a typical example of an apartment block built in the affluent *Gründerzeit* (the 'foundation' period of economic expansion in the second half of the 19thC). It is called the **Lohner-Werke-Haus** because the ground floor was originally given over to the imperial carriage company of Jacob Lohner. The firm successfully made the transition to automobiles in 1897 and later even to aircraft. **Café Monaco**, Servitengasse 4, is an inexpensive Italian restaurant (open Mon-Sat, 9 am-midnight). Turn into nearby Berggasse and you find (at No. 16) ...

③ the **Festetics Palais**, a 19thC pile built for the influential Hungarian noble family of that name by Albert Pio. It later passed to the state and housed the Austrian Export Academy, forerunner of the High School for Foreign Trade. After post-war restoration it became for a while the home of the *Handelskammer* (Chamber of Commerce), a highly influential body in Austria's system of governing through 'Social Partners' (of which the Kammer, representing industry at national level, is one). Almost opposite at No. 19 is ...

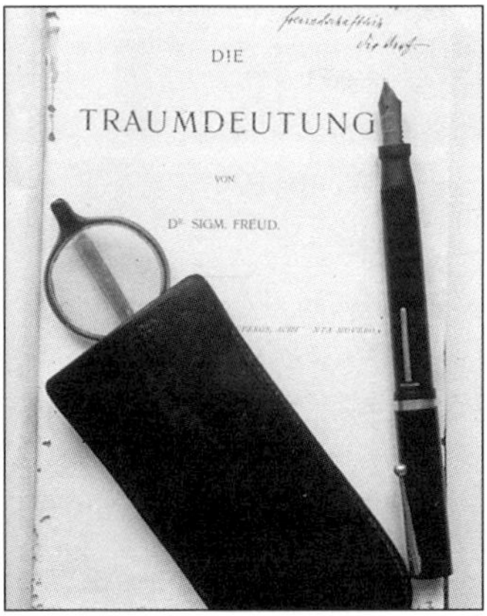

④ the **Sigmund Freud Museum**, in the house where he lived and had his practice. The Freud Society opened the museum as an act of homage in 1971. On display are various memorabilia and items from Freud's ethnographical collection; there is also a library (museum open daily, 9 am-4 pm).

Artifact in Freud Museum

The **Rudolfshof** ⑤ by Theophil Hansen at Türkenstrasse 14/Hörlgasse 15 has a glass-roofed courtyard with corridors overlooking it at each level (known in Vienna as a Pawlatschen House). The apartments inside were originally reserved for civil servants.

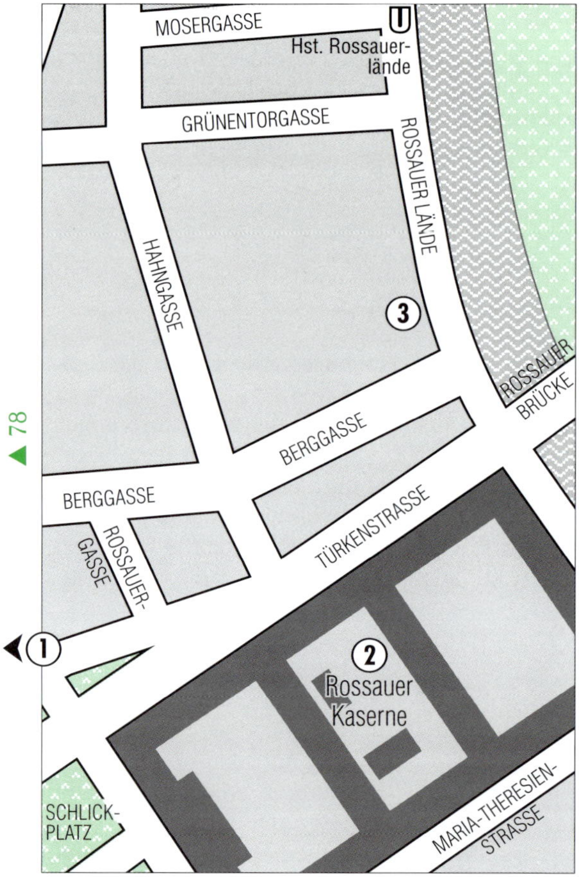
MOSERGASSE
U
Hst. Rossauer-
lände
GRÜNENTORGASSE
ROSSAUER LÄNDE
HAHNGASSE
3
ROSSAUER
BRÜCKE
BERGGASSE
BERGGASSE
TÜRKENSTRASSE
ROSSAUER-
GASSE
1
2
Rossauer
Kaserne
SCHLICK-
PLATZ
MARIA-THERESIEN-
STRASSE

▲ 78

▼ 36

① The **Schlick-palais**, at No. 25 Schlickgasse, (off map), is named after its first owner, who was also the first settler in this part of the town. Formerly it had been the *Rossauer Glacis*, meadowland preserved as a defensive strip in front of the old city. The area between Berggasse and Türkenstrasse was rechristened Neu-Wien and sprouted multi-storey apartment blocks known ominously as *Tuberkelburgen*, T.B. being the scourge of mass habitation in 19thC Vienna. General Count von Schlick's palace was actually on the site of the *Rabenstein*, the public gallows that had operated here between 1747 and the 1780s. The maintenance of law and order was also the motivation behind the erection of ...

② the **Rossauer Kaserne**, built in the 1860s. It was one of several barracks designed to remind the rebellious populace of 1848 and their heirs that force would be met with force. The barracks have an aggressively military exterior, a bit like an Italian Renaissance castle (although some claim to see similarities with Windsor). It was rumoured that the architects (a Colonel Pilhal and a Major Markl) forgot to install lavatories, but this has subsequently been exposed as a canard. Apparently the facilities were banked in the four storeys of the octagonal corner towers and took the form of *Plumpsklos* (long-drops), a medieval solution that very soon caused the fabric of the building to rot... The Rossauer Kaserne were for long the police barracks for Vienna and also the centre for driving tests, their gloomy, echoing corridors doing nothing for the morale of nervous candidates. To the west, at Rossauer Lände 5-7, is ...

③ the **former police headquarters** (*Polizeigebäude*), built by Alfred Keller in 1904 and reflecting the influence of *Jugendstil.*

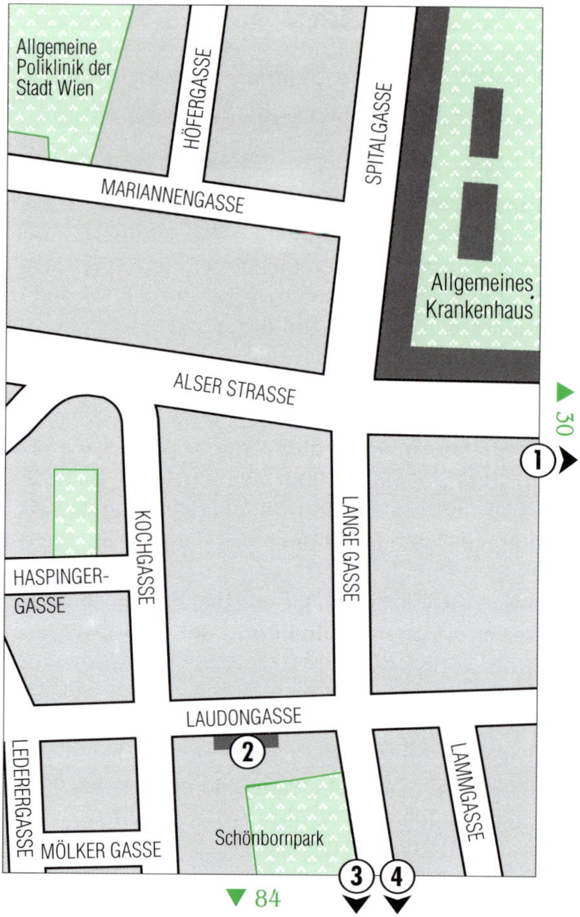

At Alser Strasse 17, on the border of Vienna's 8th and 9th Districts, is ① the **Minorite church and convent**. The original buildings were constructed between 1695 and 1727 for the Catalonian Trinitarians, known as the '*Weißspanier*' (White Spaniards) on account of their white robes, who were called to Vienna by Leopold I. (Enter via a cloister plastered with votive plaques to St Anthony of Padua.) The Emperor Joseph II dissolved the order but allowed the Minorites (whom he had dispossessed elsewhere in the city) to move in on condition that they attended to the spiritual needs of the patients in his great new hospital across the street (*see page 74*). A plaque on the wall recalls that Beethoven's funeral was held here on 29 March 1827; the line of mourners stretched all the way between his house in Schwarzspanierstrasse (*see page 77*) and the church. Schubert (who was among the mourners for Beethoven) once composed a hymn for this church ('Faith, Hope and Charity'). Make your way to ...

② Nos 17-19 – the **Schönborn-Palais**. An existing building was remodelled by Lukas von Hildebrandt after the Schönborn family acquired it in 1706. Isidor Canevale later altered it to suit neo-Classical taste. The English writer, Lady Mary Wortley Montagu, waxed lyrical about the splendour of the Baroque palace when she visited it in 1716. Since 1862 the Municipality has owned it and has turned the gardens into a (somewhat dreary) public park with playgrounds for children. The palace was occupied by the University of Agriculture, then the Supreme Provincial Court for Lower Austria, but since 1920 has housed the Folklore Museum. The exhibits include folk costumes from all regions of Austria. Turn right into Lange Gasse and you will find ...

③ the **Damian-Palais** at No. 53 (off map), distinguished by a fine wrought-iron gate. The palace was last restyled by Matthias Gerl in the early 18thC and was briefly the home of the Vienna Boys' Choir. It is now occupied by the Vienna and regional offices of the Association for the Blind and War Invalids.

④ No. 34 is the **Alte Backstube** (off map), an attractive Baroque house (1697) with a sculpted Holy Trinity over the portal. A bakery operated here uninterruptedly between 1701 and 1963. The place has now been turned into a very pleasant café and restaurant (open Tue-Sat 9am-midnight, Suns 2pm-midnight **SS**). The interior is also officially part of the District Museum and the original oven, together with various accoutrements of the baker's trade, are on display. If you are keen on noodles, try **Nudeldruckerei**, Lange Gasse 50 (**S**): open Mon-Sat 6 pm-2 am.

▲ 82

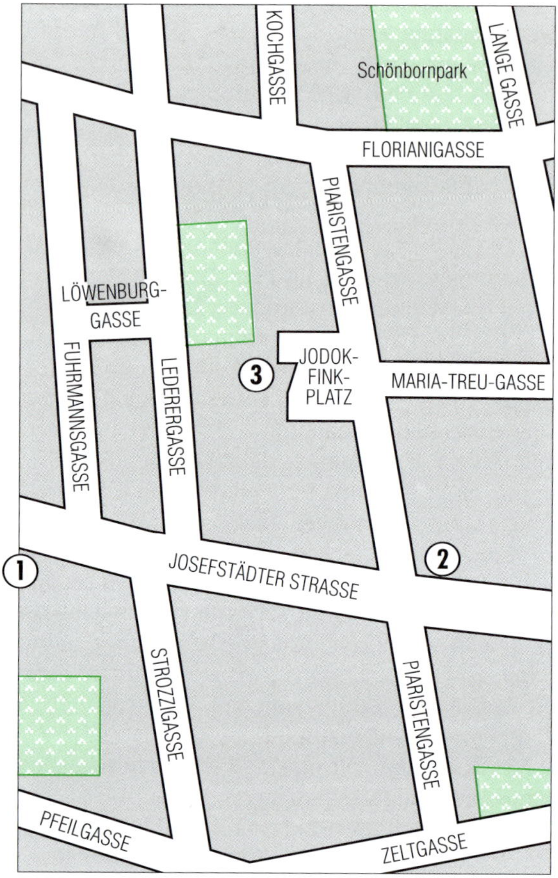

The Josefstadt (Vienna's 8th district since 1861) is one of the most elegant areas of the city and retains much of its old world charm. It was named after Emperor Joseph I (1678-1711) and the first houses were built here in 1690 (at Nos 29 and 31 in the Florianigasse). The nobility liked to locate their summer retreats in the Josefstadt, partly because it was separated from the bustle of the city until 1875 by the *glacis* (open defensive area) that stretched between the Burg and Schottentor. However the narrow streets beyond the walls of the aristocrats' palaces were evidently not so salubrious and the Josefstadt was badly hit by the cholera epidemics of 1831 and 1855.

① One such *palais* was built by Countess Maria Strozzi at **Josefstädter Strasse 39** in 1702. It later passed to the Chotek family who still owned it in the 1830s, when the portrait painter Friedrich Amerling, whose works can be seen in the Belvedere (*see page 119-21*), occupied a luxurious suite on the first floor. The *palais* is now the *Finanzamt* (tax office) for the 8th, 16th and 17th districts. Retracing your steps to No. 26 you come to ...

② the **Theater in der Josefstadt**, rebuilt by the leading architect of neo-Classicism in Vienna, Joseph Kornhäusel. (There had been a theatre on the site for many years.) At its reopening in 1822 Beethoven conducted an overture he had composed for the occasion, "looking wild and unkempt" according to one of those present. In modern times the theatre has had a reputation for high-quality productions and was one of the first to stage avant-garde drama (Strindberg and Wedekind). Its golden age followed the arrival in 1923 of the great Max Reinhardt as director. Turn right along the Piaristengasse and you arrive at Jodok-Fink-Platz and ...

③ the gracious **Piaristenkirche** (Church of the Piarists, 1753). The marvellous convex façade with rococo touches is attributed to one of the greatest architects of the Baroque in Prague, Kilian Ignaz Dientzenhofer, although Matthias Gerl and others also worked on the church. The highlight of the interior are the frescoes of biblical scenes by Franz Anton Maulpertsch, who also painted the walls of the neighbouring refectory and convent. Anton Bruckner took the practical part of his Conservatorium examination for composition on the church's organ in 1861. As the strains of the music died away and Bruckner anxiously scanned the faces of his examiners, one of them quietly remarked: "He should be examining us!" On one side of the church is the Piarists' convent and on the other is what used to be the college run by them, which is now a state *Gymnasium* (secondary school).

At Fleischmarkt 15 is ① Theophil Hansen's **Greek Orthodox Church** commissioned in 1858 by a patron of the arts of Greek extraction named Baron Sina. The lush interior, aglow with the gilded capitals of the mottled marble columns, contains frescoes in Byzantine style and a 19thC iconostasis.

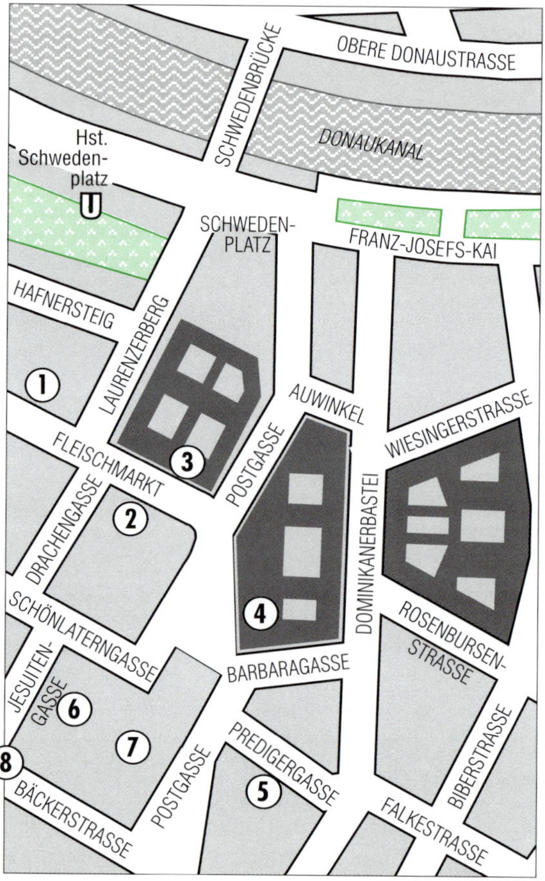

▲ 54

▶ 88

▼ 94

② The **Wiener Kammeroper** is at Fleischmarkt 24 which has an attractive *Jugendstil* auditorium. Young singers go through their paces here in adventurous, occasionally idiosyncratic productions of the operatic repertoire.

③ The **Hauptpostamt** (Main Post Office) at Fleischmarkt 19 has been under restoration for a couple of years, but it is now functioning as a modernized office in a brand new shopping mall.

④ You will find the **Ukrainian Uniate (Greek Catholic) Church** at Postgasse 10: it is usually closed. The Uniates, a sort of half-way house between Orthodoxy and Catholicism, were established during the reign of Maria Theresa and their modest little church was opened in Vienna in 1775, in what had previously been a Jesuit cloister.

⑤ The **Dominican Church** at Postgasse 4 dates to 1634 (Jakob Spatz, Cipriano Biasino and Antonio Canevale), and recalls contemporary Roman ecclesiastical architecture. The interior building contains a striking representation of St Dominicus himself by Tobias Pock, together with frescoes by Matthias Rauchmiller and rich stucco throughout. Dr.-Ignaz-Seipel-Platz is enclosed by historic buildings. On the north side is ...

⑥ the early Baroque **Jesuit Church** (1631), with a sumptuous interior by Andrea Pozzo commissioned by the pious Emperor Leopold I. The exotic barley-sugar columns are a conscious imitation of those in St Peter's in Rome. To the east is ...

⑦ the **Alte Universität**, whose history stretches back to an initiative by Rudolf IV, the Founder, in 1365. Inspired by Charles IV's great Carolinum in Prague (founded 1348), Rudolf resolved to make Vienna an equally respected seat of learning. However, the Pope withheld permission for the all-important Theological Faculty until 1384. The lecture halls remained in use until the revolution of 1848, after which the various disciplines were dispersed around town, to be reunited when the 'new' university was opened on the Ringstrasse in 1884 (*see page 33*). Opposite the university is ...

⑧ the late Baroque gem of the **Akademie der Wissenschaften** (Academy of Sciences), built to a design by Nicholas Jadot de Ville-Issy (1755). This housed the Faculty of Jurisprudence and was also used for ceremonies such as the installation of the Rector and the awarding of degrees.

① At Oskar-Kokoschka-Platz 2/Stubenring 3 is the **Hochschule für Angewandte Kunst** (School of Applied Art, 1877), originally located in the Museum of Applied Art next door (*see page 97*). Heinrich Ferstel designed this separate neo-Renaissance building for the school and a further wing was built after the Second World War. The next building along, Stubenring 1, is ...

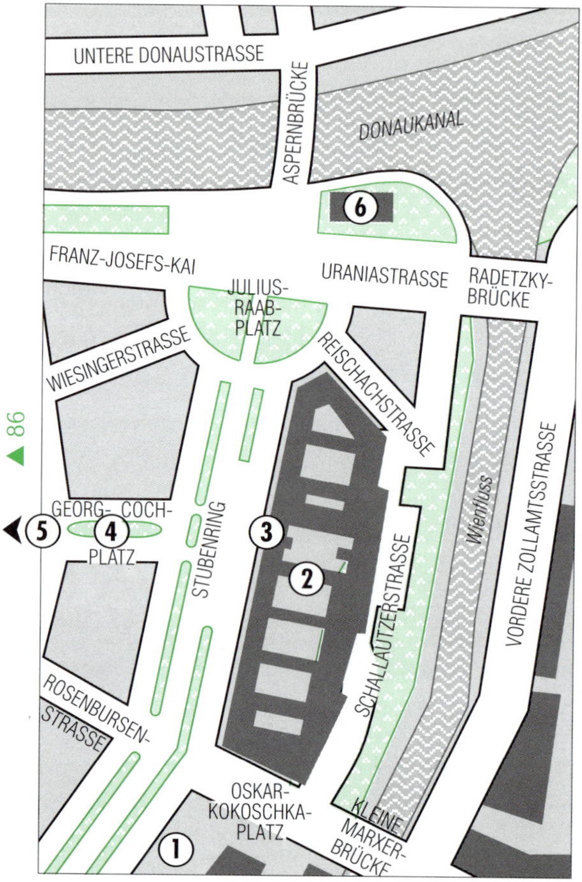

▼ 96

② Ludwig Baumann's bombastic neo-Baroque Ministry of War, now the **Regierungsgebäude**, accommodating several ministries, but not Defence. It was completed in 1913, an image of military might that was almost immediately rendered nugatory by the destruction of Austria's army in the next four years. The façade is crowned by an enormous copper eagle with trophies. In front of the building is ...

③ Caspar von Zumbusch's equestrian **statue of Field Marshall Radetzky** (1766-1858), originally erected to front the previous War Ministry, Am Hof. Reliefs on the plinth show the hero of the Italian wars (1848-49) with his generals; an inscription by the playwright Franz Grillparzer reads: 'Where your camp is, there is Austria!' Radetzky was Austria's greatest 19thC general and military strategist, who did much to turn the army into an effective fighting force. Across the Ringstrasse is a small square, in the middle of which is ...

④ a **monument to Georg Coch**. Coch was a bureaucrat who founded the Postal Savings Bank in Austria in the 1880s, after closely studying similar institutions in Europe, including the British version. He was lionized by the Christian Social Party which saw him as representing the financial interests of the little man against the big (Jewish-run) banks.

⑤ Otto Wagner's marvellous **Österreichisches Postsparkassenamt** (Post Office Savings Bank, (off map) was built between 1904 and 1912 and is generally regarded as one of the architect's finest works. His principle was to create structures that integrated functionalism with aesthetic effect and which were faithful to the materials used. The exterior is clad in plates of granite and marble fastened with highly visible aluminium-headed bolts. At the corners of the roof are two massive aluminium angels. The famous counter hall has a glass-panelled floor to let in light below, and a barrelled glass roof.

⑥ The **Urania** (Uraniastrasse 1), designed by Max Fabiani in 1910, was built for popular adult education on the model of a similar establishment with the same name in Berlin (1888). It still fulfils this function, and its cinemas show art films and presentations of the Viennale Film Festival.

▲ 40

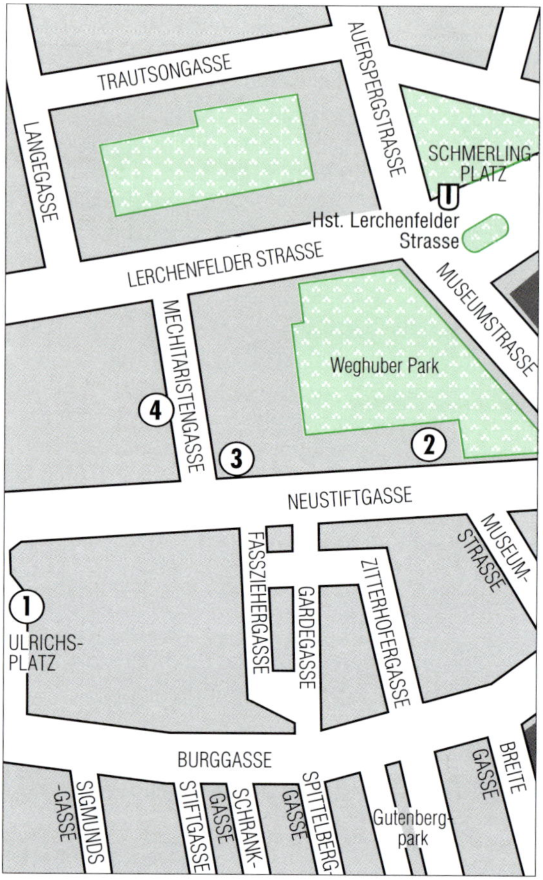

▶ 92

Tucked away on the diminutive St.-Ulrichs-Platz is ① the **parish church** dedicated to the canonised 10thC bishop who defended Augsburg against a Hungarian army and built in 1724 by Josef Reymund (off map). The impressive high altar by Paul Troger (1750) depicts St Ulrich at the Battle of Lechfeld (955). A Baroque Trinity Column stands in front of the church and period houses look on to the square. No. 2, the Old School House, is especially attractive. Within sight of the church at Kirchengasse 41 is one of Vienna's most charming small hotels, the **Altstadt Wien**, occupying the upper floors of a Baroque house (**S**). It is run by a descendant of Grete Wiesenthal, the Isadora Duncan of turn-of-the-century Vienna. Not far away is ...

② the delightful **Trautson Palace** (1709), one of the most elegantly pleasing works of Johann Bernhard Fischer von Erlach. After the Trautson family died out in 1760 the palace became the Viennese headquarters of Maria Theresa's Hungarian Lifeguards. The Hungarian government owned the palace until after the Second World War, but so neglected the fabric that there was talk of demolishing it. Since 1961 the restored building has housed the Ministry of Justice. Behind the Trautson Palace at Neustiftgasse 4/Mechitaristengasse 2 is...

③ the **Mechitharist Monastery and Church of Mary the Protectress**. This belongs to the Armenian Uniate Congregation founded in 1701 by Mekhitar (1676-1749) in Constantinople. Following a fire in the early 19thC, Joseph Kornhäusel rebuilt the cloister in 1837. It contains a monumental Nazarene painting of *The Feeding of the Five Thousand* by Ferdinand Schnorr (1839). The library possesses valuable Armenian manuscripts and at Mechitaristengasse 4 is a museum with a number of interesting items relating to the order and Armenian culture (open to visitors by appointment: tel. 93 64 17). The neo-Renaissance church is partly the work of Camillo Sitte (1873).

④ The attractive Baroque house in Mechitaristengasse was the birthplace of the musician Joseph Lanner, rival to the Strauss family in the waltz stakes.

Strauss and Lanner

① The **Volkstheater** (1889) at Neustiftgasse 1/Museumstrasse 2A is one of the many theatres built in the second half of the 19thC by the very successful partnership of Ferdinand Fellner and Hermann Hellmer. Across Museumstrasse at No. 12 is ...

▲ 42

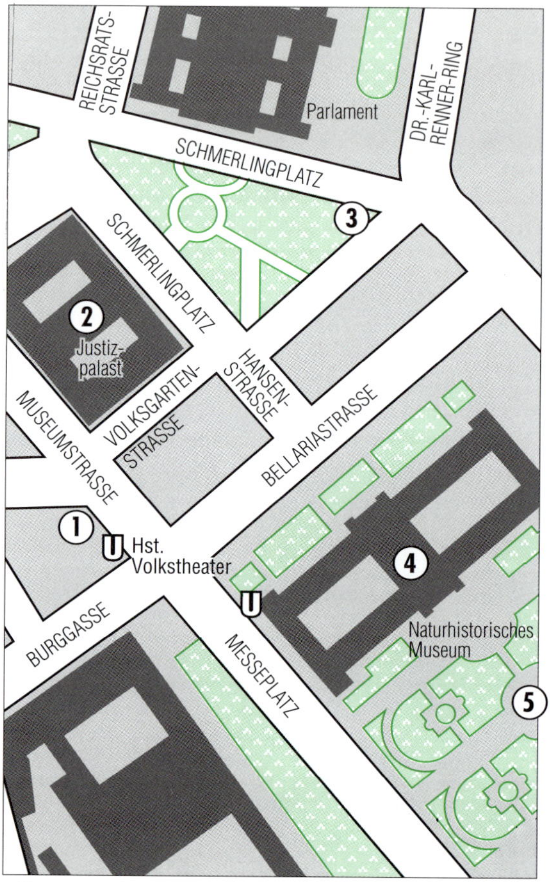

◀ 90

▶ 58

▼ 98

② the **Justizpalast** (Law Courts), a huge and gloomy product of the Ringstrasse era (1881) built by Alexander Wielemann. In 1927, after a miscarriage of justice connived at by the Christian Social government, rioting Social Democratic supporters set fire to the Justizpalast, destroying a large part of it. This proved to be the curtain-raiser for Civil War that broke out in the 1930s. On Schmerlingerplatz is ...

③ the **Monument to the Republic**. The three busts here are of socialist luminaries of the First Republic: Jakob Reumann, Mayor of Vienna from 1919 to 1923; Viktor Adler, the legendary leader of the Social Democrats, and Ferdinand Hanusch, Minister for Social Affairs in the first government after the First World War. Under the Dollfuss regime the monument was removed (1934) and only reinstated in 1948.

④ The **Natural History Museum** at Burgring 7 was part of the German architect Gottfried Semper's ambitious plan for an Imperial Forum, which was to have been linked across the Ring to the Neue Hofburg (*see pages 59 and 61*). The display is typical of 19thC taste, but it has a certain charm and is trying to adapt itself to contemporary expectations, for instance by staging a show of teddy bears that included a number of amiable-looking creatures lent by VIPs. It is open Wed-Mon, 9 am-6 pm. Between the two great museums is a pleasant park (Maria-Theresien-Platz) dominated by ...

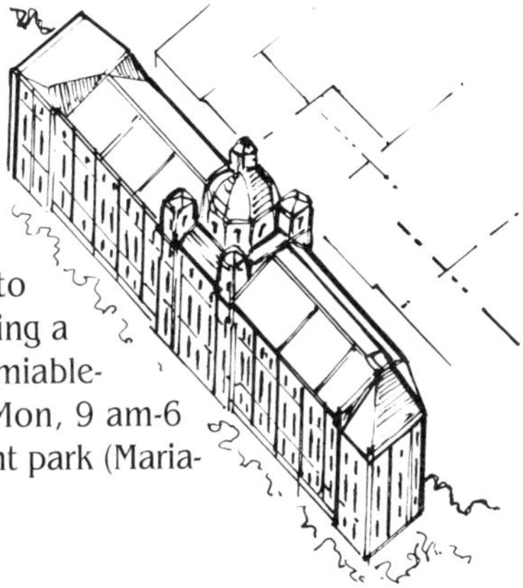

⑤ the huge **Monument to Maria Theresa**, erected in 1888 and designed by Caspar von Zumbusch. It is naturalistically conceived, but also harks back to the self-conscious rhetoric of the Baroque era. The Queen is seated on a throne; a sceptre in her left hand rests on the famous Pragmatic Sanction (1713), by means of which her father, Charles VI, had sought to legitimize her claim to the succession. Around her are equestrian statues of her greatest generals – Laudon, Traun, Khevenhüller and Daun. Standing between them are her leading administrators – Kaunitz and others. Also featured are scientists and musicians (Gluck, Haydn, the young Mozart).

To the east of Parkring is ① the delightful **Stadtpark**, laid out in 1862-63 on the initiative of Mayor Andreas Zelinka. The picturesque, landscaped park was designed by Rudolf Siebeck and the painter Josef Selleny. At the southern end is the Kursalon (*see page 108*), and to the north of that ...

② the **Johann Strauss Monument**. This is the best-known picture-postcard image of Vienna and shows the waltz-king dreamily in action; a marble arch with reliefs of figures, evidently entranced by his music, frames him like an aureola. Edmund Hellmer's florid work was unveiled in 1921 and has recently reacquired its full tinselly tastelessness since the Strauss figure was regilded. More pleasing is ...

Schubert

③ the **Bruckner Monument** further north, a naturalistic bust by Viktor Tilgner (1899). Beyond that, nearer the Ringstrasse, is...

④ the **Schubert Monument**, erected on the initiative of the Viennese Male Voice Choir in 1872. On the other side of Parkring is Dr.-Karl-Lueger-Platz, named after the most successful local politician in the history of Vienna. He came to power as a result of the widening of the franchise in the 1880s to include the *5-Gulden Männer* (those who paid five gulden in tax). The handsome Lueger – "*der schöne Karl*" as he was known – led the newly-founded Christian Social Party, which defended the interests of the small trader and *petit bourgeois* who felt exploited by the wealthy and corrupt Liberals.

⑤ Josef Müllner's **monument to Lueger**, unveiled in 1926 but completed ten years earlier, should have been set up in front of the City Hall; however, the Social Democrats, by then in power, were having none of that. Venture into ...

⑥ **Café Prückl** on the north side of the square (Stubenring 24), an old Ringstrasse establishment (**S**). It had a long tradition of cabaret and satire, performed in its cellar. It is now chiefly an atmospheric relic where pensioners play cards in the slack hours between meals, and piano music provides background entertainment in the evenings (open daily 9 am-10 pm).

⑦ Parkring 8 is the **Deutschmeister-Palais**, built by Theophil Hansen in 1868 for the head of the Teutonic Knights. It was formerly the OPEC headquarters, the scene of the celebrated hostage drama in 1975. At Parkring 12 is ...

⑧ the **Gartengebäude**, part of which is the **Hotel am Parkring** (**SS**). The latter's roof-top restaurant, **Himmelstube**, is renowned for its food (**SSS**) and its view.

⑨ The **Marriott Hotel** is at 12A (**SS/SSS**), occupying the part of the Gartengebäude site left unexploited; its aluminium façade harmonizes reasonably well with the 19thC Ringestrassen style, and touches such as the plashing fountain in the lobby enhance its air of luxury.

Heumarkt, the old hay market, runs along the east side of the Stadtpark. ① **No. 7 Am Heumarkt** is a fine apartment block in neo-Classical style (J. Dallberg, 1808, off map). Its two pleasant inner courtyards are planted with trees.

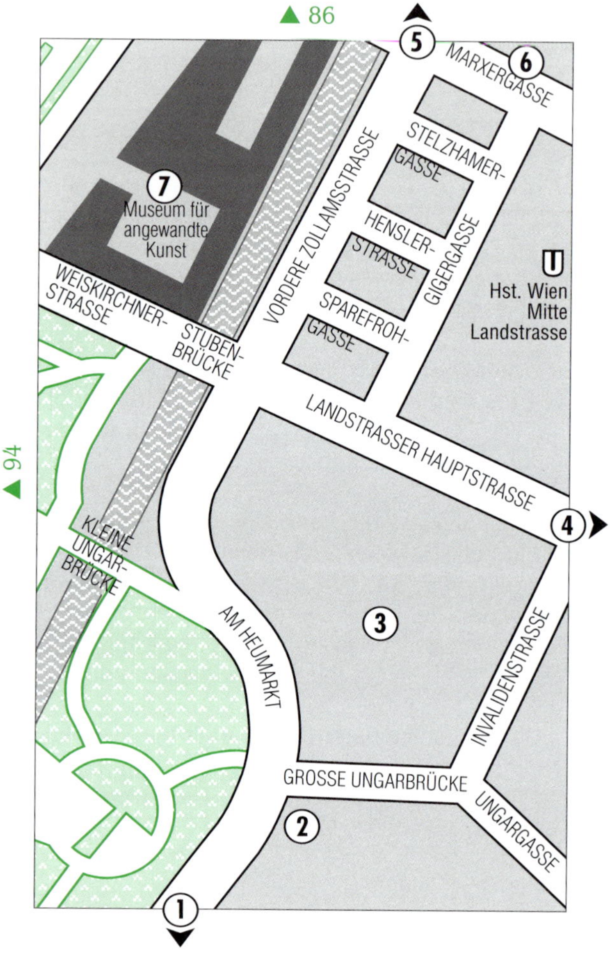

② No. 1 Am Heumarkt is the **Hauptmünzamt** (Mint), another neo-Classical building by Paul Sprenger (1838). Am Heumarkt runs into ...

③ the busy **Zentrum am Stadtpark**, a somewhat amorphous area of modern rebuilding bounded by Am Heumarkt, Invalidenstrasse, and Landstrasser Hauptstrasse. It includes a huge and depressing shopping centre and Bahnhof Wien Mitte (Vienna Central Railway Station). Also here is the City Air Terminal, which in turn is attached to the Hilton Hotel (Landstrasser Haupstrasse 2a, **SS**).

Stadtpark

④ At Landstrasse Hauptstrasse 4A is the Baroque **church and convent of the Elisabethan nuns** (1710, altered 1749; off map). Because of its nursing activity the convent escaped dissolution by Joseph II and was even enlarged between 1796 and 1799. The Vordere Zollamtsstrasse is to the west;

⑤ at No. 9 (Marxergasse 2, off map) is the **Regierungsgebäude** (Government Building), formerly the Naval Department of the War Ministry. Plaques on the wall show the coats-of-arms of the Adriatic ports of the Austro-Hungarian Empire. The graceless neo-Baroque building was erected in 1912 around the same time as the nearby War Ministry (*see page 88*). It is now the Head Office of the Federal Forestry Commission.

⑥ No. 3 is the former **Finanzlandesdirektion** (Imperial Commerce Centre, off map), erected under Ferdinand I and designed in neo-Renaissance style by Paul Sprenger. The modern building next to it at Radetzkystrasse 2 is the pompous and overblown **Bundesamtsgebäude** (Government offices, Peter Czernin, 1986). Florid sculptures by Anton Hanak front this exercise in Post-Modern excess, but at least it's startlingly colourful. Opposite No. 3 is the **Zollamtssteg**, an art nouveau bridge that crosses the River Wien just before it flows into the Donau Kanal. West of Vordere Zollamtsstrasse is the Hochschule für angewandte Kunst (*see page 88*) and next to it ...

⑦ the neo-Renaissance **Österreichische Museum für Angewandte Kunst** (Austrian Museum of Applied Art, Stubenring 5) built by Heinrich Ferstel in 1871. The museum has recently undergone massive and much-needed restoration and a glass-and-steel link between the building's two separate parts has been added. The permanent collection includes ceramics and artefacts from Europe, East Asia and the Orient, as well as glass, jewellery and furniture. It is open Tues-Sun 10am-6pm (to 9pm Thur).

▲ 92

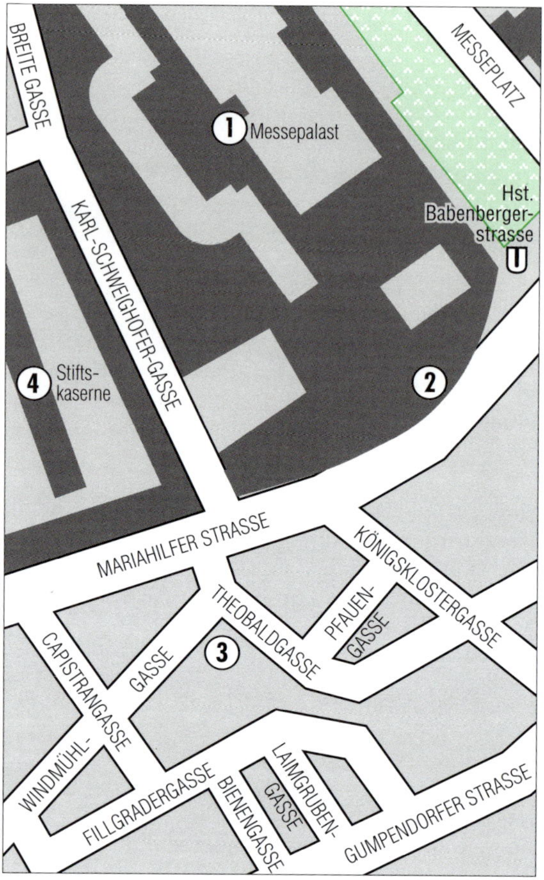

▶ 100

▲ 110

① The former **Hofstallungen** (Imperial Stables) became the **Messepalast** in 1921, used at first for the Vienna Trade Fair and subsequently for other exhibitions and events. The huge complex of buildings (354 m long) was designed by Johann Bernhard Fischer von Erlach and finished in 1723 by his son, Joseph Emanuel. Contemporaries were very critical of the building, complaining that its height was insufficient for its length. Although it lacks the customary von Erlach grandeur, it was certainly practical, accommodating not only the personal quarters of the *Oberstallmeister* and his officials, but also enough stabling for 600 horses, together with carriage sheds and a hunting armoury. The Wiener Festwochen (Vienna Arts Festival) now also uses the

Messepalast

Messepalast for performances, but even greater things are planned. The idea is to turn it into a futuristic complex of exhibition halls, including a multi-media forum, a museum of the history of ideas and a Museum of Modernism in Austria. Turn right at the south-eastern end of the Messepalast and you will find yourself in Mariahilfer Strasse.

② The **Tabakmuseum** (Tobacco Museum, open Tue-Fri 10 am-5 pm, Sat, Sun 10 am-2 pm is at No. 2. South of Mariahilfer Strasse, at Windmühlgasse 3, is ...

③ the **Laimgrubener Pfarrkirche hl. Josef** (Parish Church of St Joseph in the Laimgrube). The curious name comes from the *Lehmboden*, the loamy soil of the area that was once covered with vineyards, and that also supplied the city with bricks. The site of the church was occupied by Minorites and Franciscans in the Middle Ages; their convents were destroyed in the Turkish siege of 1529. In 1562 the land was given to Reichsherold Johann von Francolin, on condition that he build windmills (hence the name of the street). Instead he built apartments. Under Joseph I a new church was built but deconsecrated in 1797. There was for a while a barracks here, a prison and a 're-education institution for young noblemen', for privileged young men who had turned to crime. The Stiftskirche and Garnisonkirche zum hl. Kreuz (Garrison Church of the Holy Cross, Stiftgasse/Mariahilfer Strasse 24, off map) is thought to have been designed by Joseph Emanuel Fischer von Erlach (1739). The dramatic stucco scenes in the raised side-niches of the interior depict the Passion of Christ and date from the 18thC. Turn right off Mariahilfer Strasse and come to ...

④ the walls of the **Stiftskaserne**. This former academy only became a barracks when it was enlarged in Franz Joseph's time (1850).

▲ 58

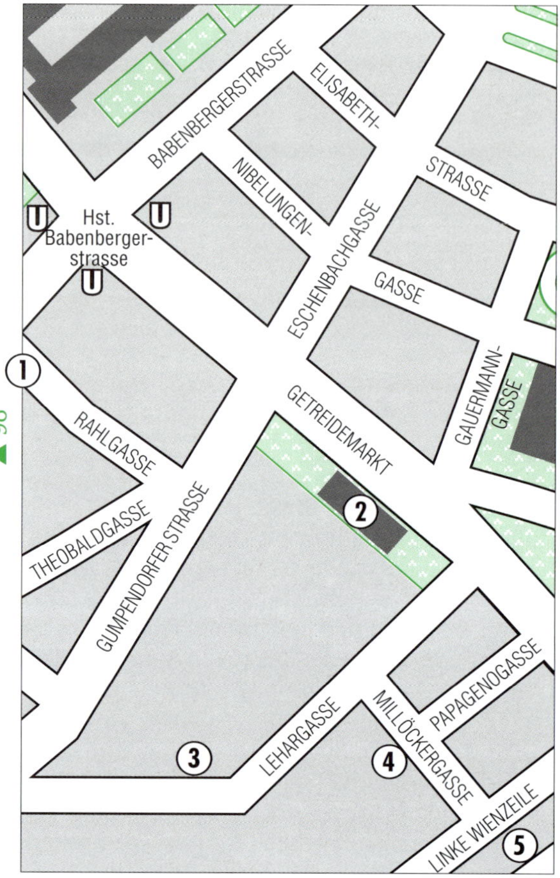

▲ 98

▲ 102

On the steps which descend from Mariahilfer Strasse to Rahlgasse is ① an attractive fountain by Anton Wagner known as the **Gänsemädchen-Brunnen** (Goose-girl Fountain, 1866). It features a girl driving a goose with a stick, while two other geese double as water spouts for the octagonal basin. The fountain was originally put up in the Inner City on Brandstätte, the historical site of the goose market. It arrived at its present location in 1886. Parallel to Rahlgasse is the Getreidemarkt (formerly the Corn Market).

② No. 9 is the **Chemical Institute** of the Technical University. Colonel Pilhal, joint architect of the Rossauer Kaserne (*see page 81*), also designed this building, which started life as the home of the Imperial Committee on Military Technology. Turn to the south off the Getreidemarkt into the Lehárgasse, and make your way to ...

③ Nos 6-8, the **Kulissen-und-Dekorationsdepot**, where scenery for the state theatres is stored. Gottfried Semper and Karl von Hasenauer designed this vast depot, built in 1877, and probably the only building in the city whose walls are still pocked with bullet marks from the Second World War. Retracing your steps, a right turn takes you into Millöckergasse, where you can see ...

④ the **Papageno Door** of the **Theatre an der Wien**. The extruding middle section of this is topped by charming rococo figures – Emanuel Schikaneder as Papageno (the part he created from his libretto and Mozart's music in *The Magic Flute*), with frolicking children beside him. The entrance to the theatre is round the corner at Linke Wienzeile 6. The original building, designed by Theodor Jäger and built by his son (1801), was Schikaneder's own theatre, replacing his Theater im Freihaus in Wieden, which had to be closed because of fire risk. Beethoven's *Fidelio* had its première at the Theater an der Wien in 1805 before an audience packed with officers of the occupying French army. It was for long the main venue for operettas and now stages the 20thC equivalent in the form of musicals. (*Cats* ran for several years to packed houses.) Immediately across the Linke Wienzeile from the theatre is ...

⑤ the famous **Naschmarkt**. This colourful market was established on land won from water after the bricking-in of the River Wien. It is packed with stalls selling fresh produce and the adjacent *Stehbeisln*, where you can eat tasty snacks standing up. The most enticing delicatessen are those selling Turkish, Greek or Levantine specialities. At the western end there is a *Flohmarkt* (second-hand market) on Saturday mornings.

The **Staatsoper** (State Opera House) ① was designed in neo-Renaissance style by August von Siccardsburg and Eduard van der Nüll and built between 1861 and 1869. The façade facing the Ringstrasse boasts an elegant two-storeyed loggia with open arcades. In the foyer is Rodin's bust of Gustav Mahler, the much-intrigued-against director of the opera between 1897 and 1907. Mahler was a ferocious disciplinarian who did much to raise artistic standards, sometimes in the teeth of conservative opposition. "Tradition," he memorably observed, "is just another word for sloppiness". This remark was directed both at audiences (who treated the opera as a coffee-house) and at performers (who paid a claque – a band of hired applauders). The opera was one of the most criticized buildings of the Ringstrassen era, however.

▲ 60

▲ 100

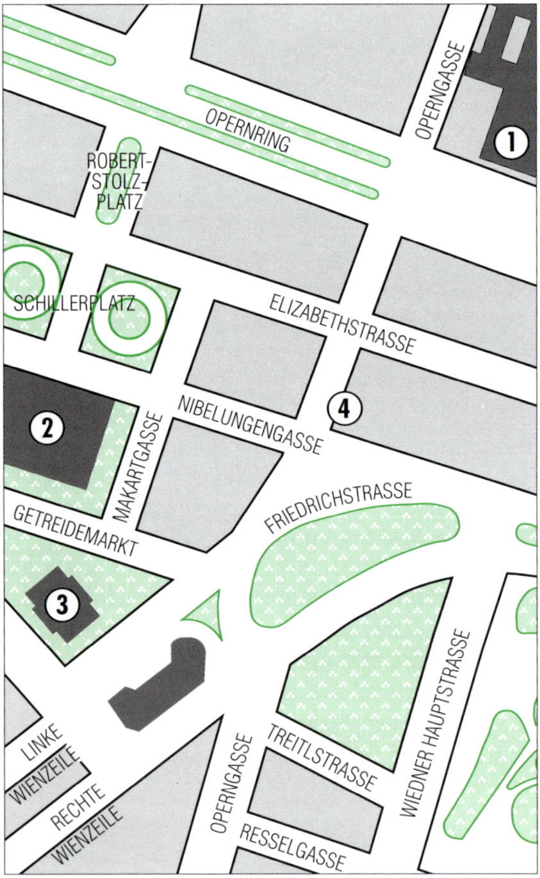

▶ 104

▼ 112

When the Emperor himself added a mildly slighting remark, the unfortunate Van der Nüll committed suicide and Siccardsburg died soon afterwards. Franz Joseph was deeply shocked and from then on confined his public comments, no matter what the occasion, to his anodyne and much-quoted formula: "*Es war sehr schön, es hat mich sehr gefreut*" ("It was very nice; I was very pleased with it"). Across the Ring is ...

② the **Akademie der Bildenden Künste** (Academy of Fine Arts), built as an Italian Renaissance palace by Theophil Hansen at the end of the 1870s. The interior has an interesting picture gallery – usually open 10 am to 2 pm, with longer hours on Wednesdays. Hitler wanted to study here but was turned down in 1907 because the work he submitted with his application was deemed too shoddy. Cheekily built virtually under the rear windows of the Academy is Josef Maria Olbrich's **Secession** building ...

③ (Friedrichstrasse 12). This was to be the exhibition hall for those who seceded from the Viennese Society of Fine Artists (almost all Academy-trained) and rejected what the academicians stood for in art. The industrialist Karl Wittgenstein (father of the philosopher Ludwig Wittgenstein) financed the building. Above the entrance in gold lettering is the Secession's slogan, composed by the critic Ludwig Hevesi: *Der Zeit ihre Kunst; der Kunst ihre Freiheit* (To the age its art; to art its freedom). Above that is a marvellous globe of gilded laurel leaves (the 'golden cabbage' as the Viennese affectionately dubbed it).

On the corner of Friedrichstrasse and the Operngasse is the **Café Museum (S)**, ④, which was one of the most celebrated works of Adolf Loos when it opened in 1899. Unfortunately, none of the original fittings remain and Loos's design really only survives in the plain façade. It was a favourite meeting-place for artists and writers (contemporaries called it 'Café Nihilismus'); the architect conceived it as a place appropriate to the social and business discourse of the modern man. Gone were the cosy private niches for whispered intimacies of the old-fashioned cafés. Instead chairs were light and portable, enabling discussion groups to form and dissolve spontaneously.

Facing the Staatsoper at Kärntner Strasse 51 is the **Todesco-Palais**, ①, built for the banker Moritz von Todesco in 1864 by Ludwig Förster and Theophil Hansen. The palace used to be the seat of the Österreichischen Volkspartei (the centre-right Austrian People's Party) but falling revenues have forced them to vacate it. On the corner of the Ringstrasse at Kärntner Ring is ...

▲ 64

▲ 102

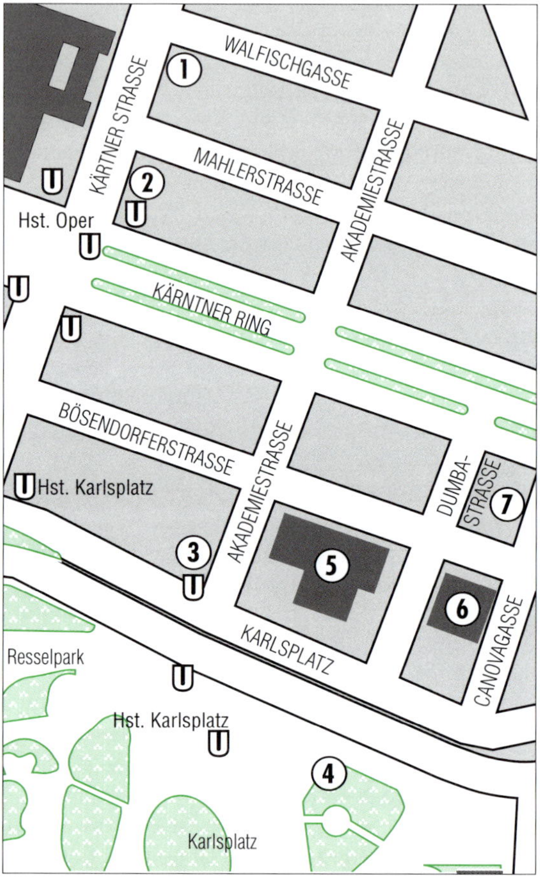

▶ 106

▼ 114

② the **Hotel Bristol (SSS)**, one of the most distinguished of the old-style Viennese hotels which has built up a reputation for its food. In particular its *Korso* restaurant (Mahlerstrasse 2, **SSS**), presided over by chef Reinhard Gerer, wins accolades as the best establishment in town (prices to match). It is open Sunday to Friday, noon to 2 pm and 7 pm to 11 pm, Saturday 7 pm to 11 pm; closed for lunch in July and August. In the same street the **Kervansaray-Hummerbar, SSS** (Mahlerstrasse 9) has Vienna's best-known fish restaurant on the first floor and offers international and Turkish specialities on the ground floor; (open Monday to Saturday, noon to 3 pm and 6 pm to 1 am). If you cross the Ring from the Hotel Bristol and take the second left into the main artery heading towards Lothringer Strasse, you come to the **Handelsakademie der Wiener Kaufmannschaft**...

③, (Karlsplatz 4), a school of commerce founded by industrialists in 1857. Ferdinand Fellner designed this new home for them in 1862 and it was enlarged in 1908. Flanking the main entrance are two suitably inspirational sculptures by Josef Cesar (1862): to the right, Christopher Columbus, to the left Adam Smith. Nearby on Karlsplatz are two graceful **Stadtbahnpavillons** ④ (Pavilions for the City Transit Railway) by Otto Wagner, who designed all the railway's architectural infrastructure between 1894 and 1901. Returning to the north side of the traffic artery via the underground passageway, you come to ...

⑤ the **Künstlerhaus** (Artists' House) at Karlsplatz 5. It was built by August Weber as the official exhibition hall for the Association of Fine Artists in 1868. Statues of eight of the world's greatest painters are ranged along the façade. Today it is used for important exhibitions, mostly staged by the Vienna Historical Museum. Just to the east of it is...

⑥, Theophil Hansen's **Musikvereinsgebäude** (Concert Hall of the Musical Society) (1869). Even more than the Staatsoper, this is the musical heart of Vienna. The 'golden hall' with its gilded caryatids and coffered ceiling can lay claim to being the most pleasing concert venue in Europe, added to which the acoustics are near-perfect. On New Year's Day the Wiener Philharmoniker plays a traditional programme of Viennese lollipops in the Musikverein, a concert that is broadast all over the world. The **Imperial Hotel** ...

⑦ built as a palace for the Duke of Württemberg in 1863, is now the Staatshotel where visiting dignitaries are put up. Its previous guests include Richard Wagner and Adolf Hitler.

Schwarzenbergplatz was laid out by Heinrich Ferstel according to a unified concept in the 1860s, the idea being to provide a frame of noble palaces around the focal point of the Schwarzenberg Monument. The latter was erected in honour of the victorious commander of the alliance against Napoleon in 1813-1814, Field Marshal Karl Philipp, Fürst zu Schwarzenberg – see ⑤ *page 107.* On the corner of Schubertring is the **Erzherzog-Ludwig-Viktor-Palais** – see ④ *page 107.* At No. 4 on the same side, beyond Lothringerstrasse is ① the **Haus der Industrie** (1909) with an inscription on the façade: 'Dedicated to the industry of Austria'. This palace was the headquarters of the four-power Allied Commission just after the war, and it was here that many of the details of the *Staatsvertrag* (State Treaty) that liberated Austria were thrashed out. On the opposite side of the square at No. 7 is...

▲ 68

◀ 104

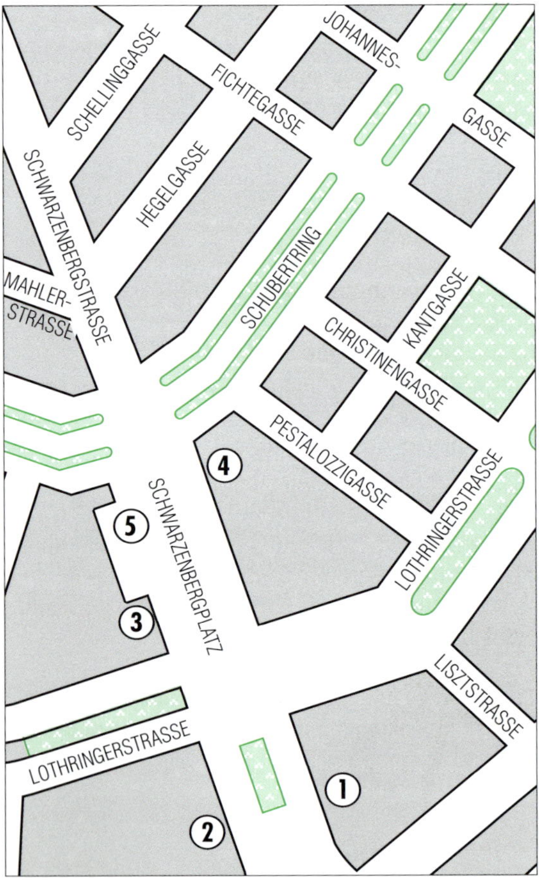

▶ 108

▼ 116

② the neo-Baroque **Haus der Wiener Kaufmannschaft** (Viennese Chamber of Commerce), 1905. On the balustrade along the front of the roof are allegorical representations of Hermes (God of commerce, of roads, of good luck – and of thieves), and of his mother Maja, together with an Atlas bearing a globe. At No. 15 is ...

③ the **Ofenheim-Palais** (1868), now housing the Zürich Kosmos Insurance Company. Viktor Ofenheim, for whom the palace was built, was the General Director of the Lemberg (Lvov) – Czernowitz Railway in Galicia. The Viennese nicknamed the palace 'Sorgenburg' (castle of woe) after the spectacular trial of its owner in 1873 for allegedly manipulating the market in railway shares. On the corner of Schwarzenbergplatz itself is ...

④ the **Ercherzug-Ludwig-Viktor-Palais** (Schwarzenbergplatz 1), built in 1869 by Heinrich Ferstel in Italian Renaissance style for Franz-Josef's youngest brother. This was the first building to be erected on the freshly laid out square. Ludwig Viktor, also known as 'Bubi' and 'Luzivuzi' was a notorious rake, homosexual and transvestite. After a scandal when he had his ears boxed by a young man he was trying to seduce in the public baths, Franz Joseph banned him to the country. On the middle of Schwarzenbergplatz is ...

⑤ the **monument to Field Marshal Prince Karl Philipp zu Schwarzenberg**, the 'Victorious commander of the allies against Napoleon in 1813 and 1814', as the inscription says. The equestrian statue is by Julius Hähnel and was unveiled in 1867. The rest of the square (see page 106) is dominated by Ringstrassen palaces belonging to large concerns and institutions. There is a MacDonald's at the north-west end and next to it a highly recommended self-service (**S**) known as *Naschmarkt*, which has a congenial sitting area and a substantial menu. It is open Monday to Friday, 6.30 am to 9 pm; weekends 9 am to 9 pm.

At the south-east end of the Stadtpark on the corner of Parkring and Johannesgasse is the **Kursalon**, ①, built by Johann Garben in 1867. This was a venue for 'promenade concerts' given in the Ringstrassen era by Eduard Strauss (the youngest of the famous musical family), and was a place for the fashionable to see and be seen. Johannesgasse runs down to Am Heumarkt.

▲ 68

▲ 104

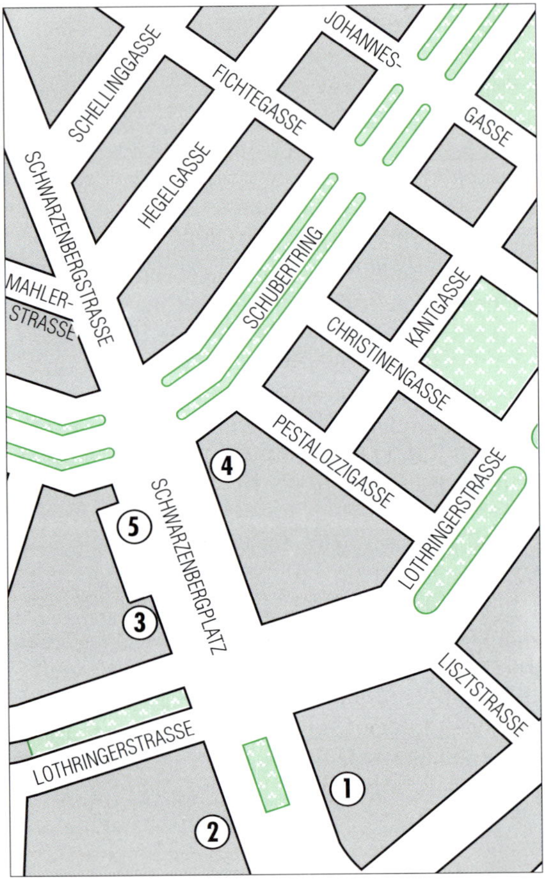

▲ 108

▼ 116

② The **Inter-Continental Wien, SSS** (1964) is at Johannesgasse 28, a building marginally more ugly than the nearby Hilton. The hotel's **Vier Jahreszeiten** restaurant (**SSS**), however, earns nothing but praise, both for the imaginative menus and the wine-list. The restaurant is open daily, noon to 3 pm and 7 pm to midnight. It is closed for Saturday lunch and Sunday dinner. At the other end of the catering spectrum, you can try ...

③ the neighbouring **Gmoa-Keller, S** at Am Heumarkt 25, behind the Konzerthaus. This place has a cult following in Vienna as it is remarkably good value. It is run by two formidable sisters of Hungarian origin who prefer their regulars and even (it is claimed) once barred the door to the current Austrian Chancellor 'because they didn't like the cut of his jib'. (Open Monday to Saturday, 8.30 am to 10 pm).

The **Salesianergasse,** ④, (a continuation of the Johannesgasse) is a narrow street leading off Am Heumarkt and was once called 'Waaggasse' after the hay wains that used it for access to the market. Its west side consists entirely of Biedermeier houses, mostly built as apartments in the 1830s. At No. 12 is the birthplace of the poet and dramatist Hugo von Hofmannsthal (1874-1929), perhaps the most gifted of the Viennese turn-of-the-century writers. He enjoyed a long and fruitful collaboration with the composer Richard Strauss, writing the librettos for *Der Rosenkavalier, Ariadne auf Naxos* and other works. Salesianergasse supplies another footnote to history: Mary Vetsera, the lover of Crown Prince Rudolf, was discreetly watched by the secret police in her comings and goings when she lived in the street. In January 1889 she and Rudolf committed suicide together at the hunting lodge of Mayerling in the Wienerwald. Retracing your steps to Am Heumarkt and turning left, you come to the rear of ...

⑤ the **Konzerthaus,** (entrance at Lothringerstrasse 20). The theatre-builders Fellner and Helmer designed and built it in collaboration with Ludwig Baumann. It had been commissioned by the Viennese Concert Hall Society and was opened in 1913. The inscription on the façade is a quotation from Wagner's Die Meistersinger von Nürnberg: *'Ehret Eure deutschen Meister, dann bannt Ihr gute Geister'* ('Honour your German master, then will your good spirits be conjured'). At Lothringerstrasse 18 is ...

⑥ the High School for Music and the **Akademie Theater**. The latter is an outpost of the Burgtheater and tends to put on plays outside the mainstream repertoire, although in recent years the distinction has become increasingly blurred.

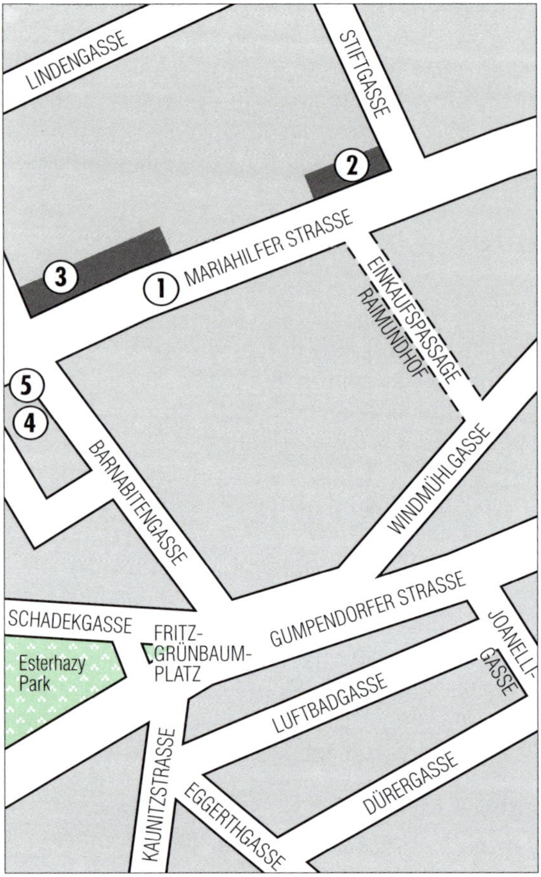

▶ 98

① **Mariahilferstrasse** is a main shopping thoroughfare of Vienna, lined with big stores (Leiner, Gerngross, Herzmansky) and smaller specialist shops for clothing, computers, music, videos and so on. A Virgin Megastore has recently been opened, to the delight of Viennese teenagers. The street was also traditionally the first stop for shoppers from the former Eastern Bloc. Even before the changes of 1989, when the Communist regime in Hungary was already in its death throes, the loosening of remaining restrictions on travel and imports resulted in floods of shoppers being bused in daily from Budapest and the border towns. The Viennese viewed this invasion with mixed feelings, ironically rechristening their Mariahilferstrasse 'Magyarhilferstrasse'. When the tidal wave of Magyars subsided, the area was stormed by Czechs and Poles as soon as their borders were opened. The greatest of the deparment stores on Mariahilferstrasse is ...

② **Herzmansky** at Nos 26-30, which has recently been modernized with no expense spared. It stands comparison with the great emporia of Paris and London. In the basement next to the food department is a gourmet's paradise of *Stüberln* (all **S**) offering everything from home-grown sausage specialities to Italian and Greek cuisine (the latter highly recommended for quality and price). At nos. 38-48 is ...

③ another large store named **Gerngross**, rebuilt and refurbished after a fire in 1979 by the distinguished architect Roland Rainer, but originally built by Adolf Wölzl in 1966. The first Gerngross on this site was built in 1905 in a luxurious mixture of late Historicism and Jugendstil by Fellner and Helmer. Contemporary commentators described it as 'palace architecture for the little man' – exactly what Adolf Loos later attacked so violently in his polemics as social pretension and *folie de grandeur.*
On the other side of the street (No. 65) is ...

④, the **Mariahilfer Pfarr- und Wallfahrtskirche Maria Himmelfahrt** (Parish and Pilgrimage Church of the Assumption of our Lady). The copy of Lukas Cranach's wonder-working icon of 'Mary the helper of mankind' (the original was in Passau, later Innsbruck) made this church an object of pilgrimage.

The **Haydn Monument** ⑤ in front of the church of Mariahilf is by a Tyrolean sculptor, Heinrich Natter, and was unveiled in 1887. The figure of Haydn, with pencil and staves in hand, is placed on a high plinth surrounded by a stone balustrade and closed by wrought-iron gates on the street side.

Haydn monument

Between the Operngasse (No. 9) and Treitlstrasse, and again at Wiedner Hauptstrasse 8, are ① the institutional buildings of the **Technical University**. On Rilkeplatz (named after the turn-of-the-century poet Rainer Maria Rilke) a **fountain** ...

▲ 102

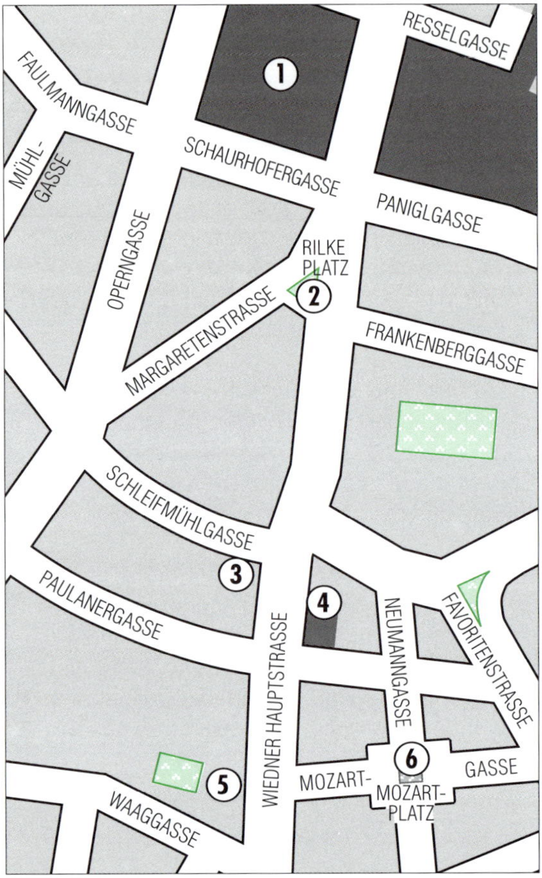

▲ 114

② was erected in 1843 celebrating the area's connection to the water main. August von Siccardsburg and Eduard van der Nüll (architects of the opera house) produced a design with some nice touches, such as the little dragons acting as water spouts; above them is the protecting angel after whom the fountain (Schutzengel-Brunnen) is named. On Schleifmühlgasse nearby, at No. 3, is ...

③ an interesting late Jugendstil house by Ernst Epstein, known as the **Paulanerhof** (1910). The Paulite Order owned property in this neighbourhood and had their **church** ...

④ on the junction of Favoritenstrasse and Wiedner Hauptstrasse. The Order was named after a 15thC Calabrian who founded the Hermits of St Francis of Assisi, but Paulites only came to Vienna in 1624, invited by Ferdinand II. At Wiedner Haupstrasse 32 is ...

⑤ the **house** where the composer Christoph Willibald Gluck (1714-1787) lived and died. There is a memorial plaque on the wall. Gluck (whose wonderful *Orfeo* and *Iphigénie en Tauride* remain in the operatic repertoire) was a breath of fresh air in the increasingly fustian music scene of Vienna when he arrived there at the age of 22. His natural style blazed a trail for the achievements of Mozart and Weber. After seeing *Alceste*, a contemporary expressed relief at the arrival of an opera with no castrati and no `coloratura caterwauling'. Moreover it was sung to an Italian libretto that frequently made sense. On the other side of the Haupstrasse, Mozartgasse brings you to Mozartplatz where ...

⑥ the **Mozart Fountain** (1905) is to be found. It shows the figures of Tamino and Pamina, hero and heroine of *The Magic Flute*, probably the opera most loved by the Viennese. Further east you come to Favoritenstrasse, where a right turn brings you at No. 15 to the imposing façade of the **Theresianum** (off map). Erected on the side of the Favorita Palace (a hunting lodge of the Emperor Matthias), the core of the present building was designed by Ludovico Burnacini and built between 1687 and 1690. After its enlargement between 1720 and 1730, Charles VI used it for lavishly staged festivities; when he died in it in 1740, his grief-stricken daughter (Maria Theresa) could never again feel happy here and decided to make Schönbrunn into her Summer Palace. She sold the Favorita to the Jesuits, on condition that they set up a college for the nobility on the premises. It has remained a seat of learning in one form or another ever since and was constantly enlarged. It now houses the Theresianum Gymnasium and the Diplomatic Academy.

▲ 104

▲ 112

▲ 116

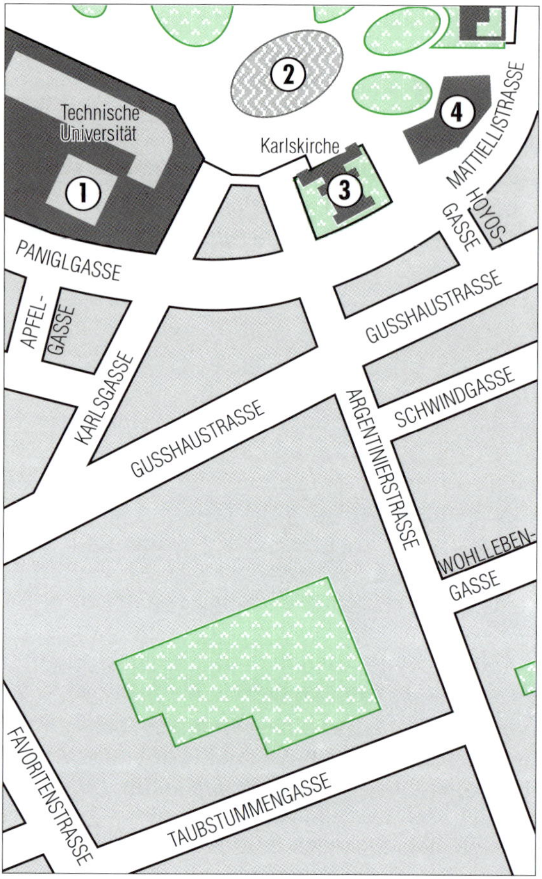

The charming Karlsplatz merges at its western end into the less than attractive region of the Resselpark and environs. At Karlsplatz 13 is ① the main building of the **Technical University** (1816). The initiative for such an institution came from the Emperor Franz I, who regarded hard sciences and technology as reasonably 'safe areas' (unlike the humanities, which had to be rigorously superintended to ensure they presented no challenge to his autocracy). But even technology could be suspect: Josef Ressel (1793-1837), whose statue by Anton Fernkorn fronts the university, invented the ship's screw; after a few tests on the Adriatic, further work on it was forbidden by the ever-alert authorities. After all, who knew what such an invention could lead to? As you walk east towards the Karskirche you will come to a large shallow basin filled with water; in the middle of this is

② **Henry Moore's 'Hill Arches'**, a sculpture he donated to the city of Vienna in 1978. (At that time Karlsplatz was being laid out anew).

③ The **Karlskirche**, dedicated to St Charles Borromeo and founded by Emperor Charles VI, is the loveliest Baroque church in Vienna. In front of it are two gigantic columns modelled on Trajan's column in Rome and topped by the Habsburg crown and eagle. Their spiralling friezes tell the story of the life of St Charles and of the miracles that occurred after his death. The saint was famous for assisting with the relief of his flock during the plague of 1576. This was why the Emperor decided to raise a church dedicated to him, following a devastating outbreak of the disease in Vienna in 1713, which killed 8,000 people. The church was designed by Johann Bernhard Fischer von Erlach and completed in 1739 by his son, Joseph Emanuel. Glimpsed through a street opening or through the trees of the park as you emerge from the U-Bahn, the Karlskirche seems absolutely magical; and even more so when illuminated at night or gleaming in the winter snow. The interior is a long oval, evoking a tremendous feeling of power and grace. In the high (72-m) cupola is Johann Michael Rottmayr's fresco of the apotheosis of St Charles and a scene showing him beseeching God to lift the plague from Vienna. In the sacristy are displayed the pluvial and cardinal's hat (made of straw) that belonged to Charles Borromeo.

④ The nearby **Historisches Museum der Stadt Wien** (Karlsplatz 8) is a depressingly uninspired building, although it is fortunately located on the periphery of the square so that it cannot detract from the impact of the Karlskirche. The contents are, however, well worth seeing and cover the city's topography, history, art and culture on three floors. It is open Tuesday to Sunday, 9 am – 4.30 pm.

▲ 106

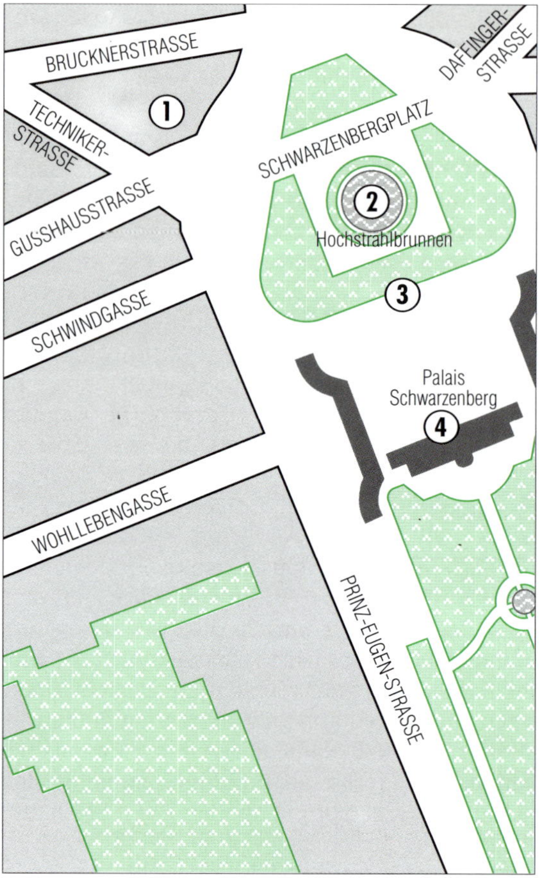

▲ 114

▲ 118

① The **French Embassy** (1909) is situated on the west side of the cobbled junction at the south-eastern end of Schwarzenbergplatz (Technikerstrasse 2). As an example of French Art Nouveau by the chief architect of the Foreign Ministry (Georges Paul Chédanne), it is unique in the Viennese cityscape. The two massive gilded reliefs at each side of the façade are allegories of Austria and France. At the heart of the junction (and obscuring the Schwarzenberg-Palais beyond) is ...

② the **Hochstrahlbrunnen** (High Jet Fountain) and...

③ the **Russian War Memorial**. The former was built by Anton Gabrielli and was ceremonially inaugurated in 1873 in the presence of the Emperor. Gabrielli, a successful contractor, financed the construction out of his own pocket to the tune of 200,000 crowns; later (1906) the fountain was illuminated. **The Russian War Memorial** has, for obvious reasons, become an object of controversy. However, a treaty exists between the Soviet Union and the Republic of Austria whereby the latter undertakes to maintain and protect the monument – a small price for the fledgling republic to pay if it helped to get the Russians off their backs in the 1950s. The Viennese were not altogether impressed by this piece of architectural rhetoric, having had first-hand experience of Russian occupation. Although the monument is officially dedicated to The Unknown Soldier, it is commonly referred to as 'The Unknown Plunderer' or 'The Unknown Rapist'.

④ **Palais Schwarzenberg** beyond is now a luxury hotel and still in possession of the family. It is a fine Baroque palace and boasted the first steam machine in Vienna which was used to work the fountains.

▲ 108

▲ 116

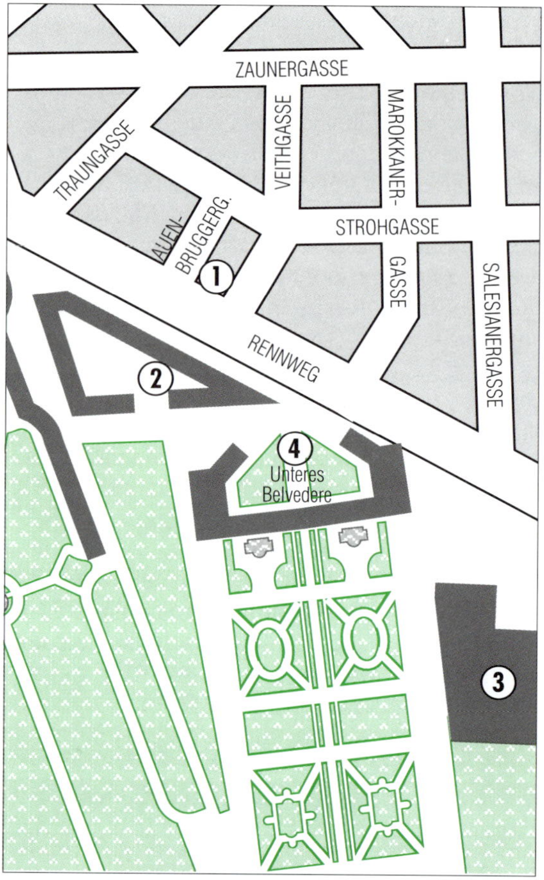

▼ 120

① The **Gardekirche** (Rennweg 5A) is also the Polish National Church in Vienna (since 1898). It has a rather simple exterior, but the oval interior is more lush, with attractive gilded decoration. The church was originally designed by Nikolaus Pacassi, the architect of Schönbrunn (see page 124-5) and subsequently altered by Peter Mollner. In 1983 the new organ was blessed by Pope John Paul during his visit to Vienna, which has no doubt improved its performance. Across the road is

② the **Orangerie** of the Belvedere Palace, where the Museum of Medieval Austrian Art is housed. If you now walk past the gateway of the Unteren Belvedere, you come to ...

③ the **Salesianerinnen-Kirche** (Rennweg 10). In 1716 the widow of Emperor Joseph I, Amalia Wilhelmine of Brunswick-Lüneburg, founded a Salesian convent here that was also to be a seminary for noble girls. She herself retired to the convent after a marriage blighted by the philandering of her husband, who had infected her with venereal disease. Her unsuccessful efforts to get her daughters, and then her son-in-law, recognized as heirs to the throne similarly blighted her widowhood after Joseph died unexpectedly young in 1711. The church (not completed until 1730) was built by Donato Felice d'Allio, and Joseph Emanuel Fischer von Erlach worked on the façade. Retrace your steps to ...

④ the **Unteren Belvedere** or Lower Belvedere, (Rennweg 6). This part of the vast complex built by Lukas von Hildebrandt for Prince Eugene of Savoy was erected between 1714 and 1716. It was designed as the business end of the palace, accommodating the administrative offices for the Prince's vast estates. Now it contains the **Austrian Baroque Museum**, the star items of which are the original of Georg Raphael Donner's Providentia Fountain (see page 67) and the extraordinary busts with grimacing faces by Franz Xaver Messerschmidt. In the marble hall is a grandiloquent ceiling fresco by Marino Altomonte showing the apotheosis of Prince Eugene, who has just smashed the Turks at the battle of Peterwardein (Serbia). Opening times for all parts of the Belvedere are the same (Tue-Sun 10 am-5 pm).

Unteres Belvedere

▲ 118

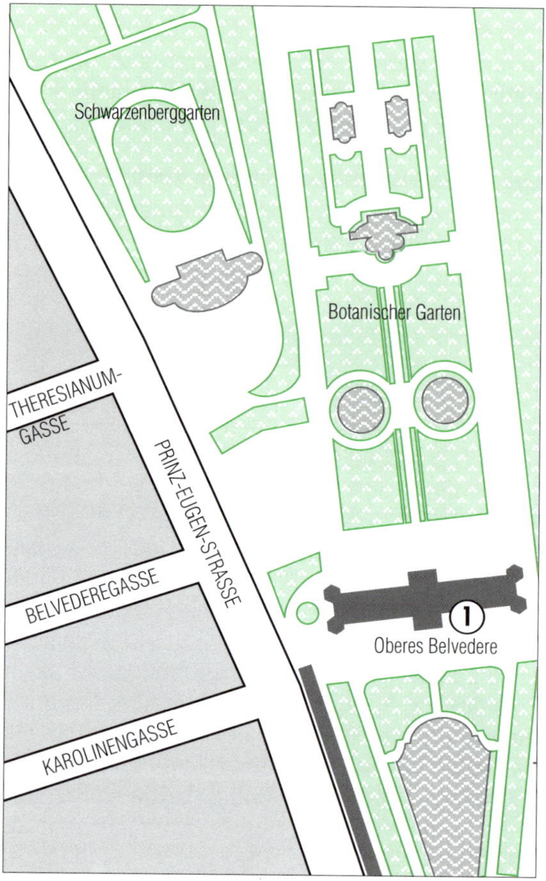

From the Unteren Belvedere you approach ① the magnificent **Oberes Belvedere** through a Baroque garden laid out by a Bavarian, Dominique Girard. This has been much reduced from its original schematic grandeur, whereby the sculpture of the western part was dedicated to Apollonian themes and that of the eastern part recalled Hercules. This reflected Prince Eugene of Savoy's double-sidedness as man of learning (with a huge library and art collection) and military hero. At the lower end of the garden, the elements in all their unpredictable workings, were sculpturally represented, while the upper end was the domaine of the gods. The now much plainer garden is still delightful for a walk and it is also worth making the small detour to visit the adjacent Alpine and Botanical Gardens (entrance from Landstrasser Gürtel or Mechelgasse 2. The Oberes Belvedere is again the work of Lukas von Hildebrandt, who was able to begin work on it when his patron had successfully negotiated to buy a slice of the neighbouring gardens of Prince Schwarzenberg. You enter the palace through the very striking *sala terrena* (originally a drive-through arcade for carriages delivering their noble charges, now the vestibule of the - see below). Stupendous Atlas figures support the vaulted ceiling with its rich stucco. If you climb the stairs to the first floor you will come to the **Festsaal** (Ceremonial Hall), clad in marble and stucco. It was here that the State Treaty liberating Austria was signed in 1955 by the representatives of the Allies - Dulles for the U.S.A., Macmillan for the U.K., Pinay for France and Molotov for the U.S.S.R. The Belvedere houses on the first and second floors the collection of the **Österreichischen Galerie** or Austrian Gallery, comprising works by Austrian artists of the 19th and early 20thC. The most popular with visitors tend to be those by Gustav Klimt, Egon Schiele and Oskar Kokoschka on the upper floor; but it is also well worth taking a look at the idealised portraits, landscapes and genre pictures on the first floor. These date from the so-called Biedermeier period (1814-1848), when Austria had two faces: that of Metternich's police state, and that of the bourgeois idyll of family life. The latter was often a kind of compensation for citizens whose lives were ordered and whose entertainment was censored by the authorities. In 1775, Joseph II moved the Imperial Picture gallery to the Belvedere, which became in 1783 the first art collection to boast a scientific catalogue and to offer free access to the public. In 1892 the pictures were transferred to the newly built Kunsthistorisches Museum on the Ringstrasse (see page 59). The palace then became the residence of the heir to the throne, Archduke Franz-Ferdinand. Up to his assassination in 1914 it was the centre of a rival court and a shadow government to that of Franz Joseph, with whom Franz-Ferdinand was on spectacularly bad terms. The building passed to the Austrian Republic after the First World War.

Oberes-Belvedere

The **Schlosstheater**, (part of the palace of Schönbrunn, on the right if you are facing the façade) was built on the orders of Maria Theresa and was primarily intended for private performances of music and dancing by her many talented children; (out of a total of 16 no less than 13 survived infancy). The little princes and princesses enjoyed the services of the most illustrious composers of the day to write music and ballets for them, (for example Christoph Willibald Gluck and Mozart's great rival, Antonio Salieri). The rococo theatre designed by Nikolaus Pacassi was remodelled in 1767 by Ferdinand von Hohenberg. When Napoleon was living in Schönbrunn during the French occupations of 1805 and 1809, the theatre was used for virtuoso concerts and performances of classical French drama. After the founding of the Austrian Republic, the Schlosstheater became the Burgtheater's second stage. From 1929 it was used for 'acting seminars' by the great director and impresario, Max Reinhardt, and it is still used for training young actors. The Wiener Kammerspiele also holds a summer season here. Adjacent to the palace on the right is ...

the **Wagenburg** (Carriage Museum). It includes an 18thC imperial coach and the hearse used at Franz Joseph's funeral in 1916. Some way to the south west of the palace in the park is ...

a magnificent iron and glass **Palmhouse** built by F. Segenschmid in 1882, the largest such construction in Europe at that time. This is close to ...

the entrance to the **Tiergarten** (zoo), which can trace its origin to the naturalist bent of the Renaissance Emperor Maximilian II, and also of Maria Theresa's husband, Franz-Stephan of Lorraine. The latter financed expeditions for bringing back animals, plants and botanical specimens from far-flung parts of the world, such items being used to enhance both the park at Schönbrunn and the imperial collection that eventually became the Natural History Museum. Schönbrunn Park itself was laid out by a Frenchman named Jean Trehet and subsequently altered by a Dutch landscape gardener, Adrian van Steckhoven. The alteration transformed it to some extent from a Baroque garden (elements of which remain in the formal parterres and stylised pruning of the trees along the *allées*) into a Romantic one. Ferdinand von Hohenburg supplied some of the ingredients for the latter, including a handy set of fake Roman ruins. It was Hohenburg who designed the park's *pièce de résistance*, namely the ...

Gloriette on the hill to the south. This is a stone pavilion surmounted by an eagle with outstretched wings, from the arcade of which there are wonderful views of the city and the palace. The Gloriette was built to celebrate the Battle of Kolin (1757), when Maria Theresa's generals inflicted a resounding defeat on her arch-enemy, Frederick II of Prussia.

In the 16thC the Emperor Maximilian II acquired a hunting reserve in the area known as Hietzing. Some one hundred years later, water with healing properties was discovered on the estate; the **ornamental fountain** built at its source gave the place its name of **Schönbrunn** (beautiful spring). In 1692 Johann Bernhard Fischer von Erlach, who was at that time architectural tutor to the future Emperor Joseph I, drew up plans for a palace at Schönbrunn that was to be grandiose enough to rival Versailles. However, the work hardly progressed because Joseph I died young and Charles VI was more interested in the hunting potential of the land than in building a palace. His daughter, Maria Theresa, created Schönbrunn as we know it today. She commissioned her court architect, Nikolaus Pacassi, to turn the existing modest hunting lodge into a noble palace which subsequently became her favourite residence. Here she lived a remarkably unstuffy family existence surrounded by her numerous progeny. The child prodigy Mozart played for her at Schönbrunn, jumping into her lap when she praised his playing and announcing to general laughter that he had decided to marry one of the princesses. Mozart's friend and mentor, Joseph Haydn, is also known to have visited the palace one day when he was still a chorister at St. Stephan's and building works were not yet complete: he received a severe wigging from the Queen for adventurously climbing over the scaffolding against her express orders. Pacassi built Schönbrunn in a rather bland Baroque style between 1744 and 1749: the building impresses more because of its size and setting than for any particular aesthetic grace. Guided tours of the rococo interiors are available daily, generally between 9 am and 5 pm, with slight variations to the timetable according to season. Highlights of the tour include: **Franz Joseph's study** (Room 4), where the aged Emperor died on November 20, 1916; the **Breakfast Room** (Room 13), which contains embroidery done by Maria Theresa's daughters; the **Mirror Room** (Room 16), where Mozart performed; the **Vieux-Laque-Zimmer** (Room 26), with black lacquer panels from East Asia; and the **Millionen Zimmer** (Room 29), so-called because it is said to have cost a million to build. It contains 260 Persian and Indian miniatures and has an elaborate gilded decoration. There is also a **chapel** – open on Sundays – with paintings by Daniel Gran and Paul Troger. The palace has recently been privatised, a deal that aroused much controversy in Austria, where the state has traditionally taken the leading role in the care and upkeep of major monuments. In the future there may be benefits for the sightseer, and in particular the **Bergl-Zimmer** (to the left of the entrance) may be made generally accessible. The latter contains exotic landscapes painted by a Bohemian artist, Johann Wenzl Bergl, and an architectural display about the successive phases of the palace's construction. Many visitors however, skip the interior altogether and just enjoy wandering around the ponds, the artificial ruins, the *allées* and the orangery of the great park.

GENERAL POINTS OF INTEREST

INDEX OF GENERAL POINTS OF INTEREST

A

B

C

D

J

K

L

M

U

V

W

Z

INDEX OF PEOPLE OF INTEREST

G

H

J

K

R

S

T

V

W

Z

STREET NAMES

INDEX OF STREET NAMES

A

B

C

D

H

I

J

K

L

M

N

O

P

R

S

T

U

V

W

Z